Library Leadership: Visualizing the Future

Edited by Donald E. Riggs

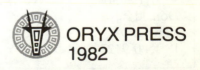

ORYX PRESS
1982

The rare Arabian Oryx is believed to have inspired the myth of the unicorn. This desert antelope became virtually extinct in the early 1960s. At that time several groups of international conservationists arranged to have 9 animals sent to the Phoenix Zoo to be the nucleus of a captive breeding herd. Today the Oryx population is nearing 300 and herds have been returned to reserves is Israel, Jordan, and Oman.

Copyright © 1982 by The Oryx Press
2214 North Central at Encanto
Phoenix, Arizona 85004

Published simultaneously in Canada

Printed and Bound in the United States of America

Library of Congress Cataloging in Publication Data
Main entry under title:

Library leadership.

   Includes bibliographical references and index.
   1. Libraries.   2. Leadership.   I. Riggs,
Donald E.
Z665.L677   020   82-2174
ISBN 0-912700-64-5   AACR2

Table of Contents

Preface

In the past few years, "leadership" has become a common word in our vocabulary. The past two U.S. presidential campaigns have, with some degree of consistency, emphasized "a change in leadership" and "new leadership." Many would agree that leadership has become one of the most magnetic words in our language.

During my search of the literature, I was appalled by the scarcity of books and journal articles on leadership in librarianship. For example, I could not find any books on the subject in the latest *Books in Print*. While perusing issues of *Library Literature* from 1975–81, to my amazement, I found fewer than five entries containing the words leadership and leader. Realizing that the library profession is noted for following, rather than "leading," the business professions in implementing modern administration/management principles and techniques, I went to *Business Periodicals Index* to check on leadership. To my surprise and gratification, for a one-year period (August 1979–July 1980), this popular index contained more than 50 entries on leadership/leaders.

Why do we have this dearth of information in the library literature concerning such a popular topic? Do libraries and their organizations not need leaders and leadership? I cannot, and will not, attempt to answer the first question. The answer to the second question is obvious. Our society demands and is entitled to strong, creative leadership for its libraries! Good management of libraries and their organizations will not be enough for the remainder of this century; they must be "led" into the twenty-first century.

The aforementioned concerns provided the rationale for this collection of essays. The authors of the 12 chapters herein have done some crystal ball gazing while predicting the events of the 80s and 90s. More importantly, they have identified the role leadership must serve during this decade and the ensuing one.

I genuinely thank all those who contributed to this work. It is my opinion that their efforts have helped to fill a gap in the professional literature.

Donald E. Riggs

Introduction

According to James MacGregor Burns, one of the strongest cravings of our time is the hunger for compelling and creative leadership. He refers to our country as lacking leadership and indeed being in a leadership crisis.[1] Historian Henry Steele Commager echoes and reinforces Burns' belief that we are experiencing a leadership crisis. He offers the following reason for this predicament:

> One of the most obvious explanations of the failure of leadership in our time is that so few of our leaders—and our potential leaders—seem to have any road map. It is hard to lead when you yourself are in a labyrinth.[2]

The alarming concern and fascination for leaders and the leadership phenomenon is of such gargantuan proportion that *Time* magazine devoted special attention to the topic in its July 15, 1974 and August 6, 1979 issues and will likely focus again on leadership in 1984.

The contributors to *Library Leadership: Visualizing the Future* were asked to address the current status of leadership in their areas of expertise and to project the impact leadership, or the lack of it, will have on their specialties in librarianship. They were asked: (1) not to project beyond the year 2000 and (2) not to devote much attention to library administration and management.

Burns defines leadership as follows:

> Leadership over human beings is exercised when persons with certain motives and purposes mobilize, in competition or conflict with others, institutional, political, psychological, and other resources to arouse, engage and satisfy the motives of followers.[3]

Administration/management in librarianship has been well-covered in the literature, while there is a noticeable scarcity of material on library leadership. Much of the recent library administration/management literature is redundant. There has been a growing danger of confusing leadership with some combination of management and conciliatory skills. These are both important, but the sum of the highest development of each does not add up to leadership.

Management and leadership are two separate hemispheres. Managers tend to work within defined bounds of known quantities, using well-established techniques to accomplish predetermined ends; the manager tends to stress means and neglect ends. The leader's task is to hold, before all persons connected with an institution or organization, some vision of what its mission is and how it can be reached more effectively. Managers may be described as being too busy doing the possible to find time to reach for the difficult or impossible. Leadership involves looking forward, as well as inward. Bennis distinguishes leadership from administration/management:

> If a leader is not careful, he will be sucked into spending all his time on the important but stifling and inevitably mundane tasks of organizational maintenance. Leadership is the capacity to infuse new values and goals into the organization, to provide perspective on events and environments which, if unnoticed, can impose constraints on the institution. Leadership involves planning, auditing, communicating, relating to outside constituencies, insisting on the highest quality of performance and people, keeping an eye out for forces which may lead to or disable important reforms. Administration is managing given resources efficiently for a given mission. Leaders question the mission. Once the leader gets sucked into the incredibly strong undertow of routine work, he is no longer leading, he is following, which he is not paid to do.[4]

In answering the question posed in his article appropriately entitled ''Where Have All the Leaders Gone?'', Bennis gives the following reasons for the disappearance and/or lack of leaders:

> They're consulting, pleading, trotting, temporizing, putting out fires, either avoiding—or, more often—taking too much heat, and spending too much energy doing both. They are peering at a landscape of ''bottom lines,''. . . . They resign. They burn out. They decide not to run or serve. They are motivating people through fear. . . . They are all characters in a dreamless society. Groping in the darkness, learning how to ''retrench,'' as if that were an art like playing the violin. And they are all scared.[5]

And who can blame them? Precisely at the time when the trust and credibility of our leaders is at an all-time low, and when survivors in leadership feel most inhibited in exercising the potentiality of power, we most need individuals who can lead. We need people who can shape the future, not just barely manage to get through the day.

Bennis states that there is no simple solution to the leadership problem. But he does give us some insights of leadership of which we should be cognizant:

1. Leaders must develop the vision and strength to call the shots. There are risks in taking the initiative. The greater risk is to wait for orders.

2. The leader must be a "conceptualist" (not just someone to tinker with the "nuts and bolts"). A conceptualist is more than an "idea man." S/he must have an entrepreneurial vision, a sense of perspective, and the time and inclination to think about the forces and raise the fundamental questions that will affect the destiny of both the institution and the society within which it is embedded.

3. The leader must have a sense of continuity and significance.

4. The leader must get at the truth and learn how to filter the unwieldy flow of information into coherent patterns. S/he must prevent the distortion of that information by over-eager aides who will tailor it to what they consider to be his/her prejudices or vanities. The biggest problem of a leader—any leader—is getting the truth.

5. The leader must be a social architect who studies and shapes what is called the "culture of work"—those intangibles that are so hard to discern but are so terribly important in governing the way people act, the values and norms that are subtly transmitted to individuals and groups and that tend to create binding and bonding.

6. The task of the leader is to lead. And to lead others s/he must first of all know him/herself. The ultimate test is the wise use of power. As Sophocles says in *Antigone:* "It is hard to learn the mind of any mortal, or the heart, till he be tried in chief authority. Power shows the man."[6]

Followers want the leader to show them the way and give them experiences which convince them that their loyalty to the group is a good thing. Leadership is not a matter of hypnosis, blandishment, or "salespersonship," nor is it a process of exploiting others for extraneous ends. It is a matter of drawing out from individuals those impulses, motives, and efforts which represent them most truly. It is a matter of directing individuals, in associated effort, toward personal power, integrated desires, and heightened sensibility. Leadership is known by the personalities it enriches. The proof of leading is in the qualitative growth of those being led, as individuals and as group members.

The leader is one who knows, with greater than average strength of conviction, what s/he wants to get done and where s/he wants to go. The world stands aside to let the leader pass.

There are times when a leader finds him/herself alone, ignored, or betrayed by other loyalties. To know when to stand valiantly alone and let time and circumstance justify one's stand is essential to the leader.

The effectiveness of a leader may depend, in part, on a given situation (geographical, economical, political, and social factors). A leader who is effective in one setting may not be as effective in another environment.

A person does not become a leader by virtue of the possession of some combination of traits; the pattern of personal characteristics of the leader must bear some relevant relationship to the characteristics, activities, and goals of the followers. Thus, leadership must be conceived in terms of the interaction of constantly changing variables. The personal characteristics of the leader and of the followers are highly stable when compared to the characteristics of the situation, which may be radically altered by the addition or loss of members, changes in interpersonal relationships, changes in goals, competition of extra-group influences, and the like. The persistence of individual patterns of human behavior in the face of constant situational change appears to be a primary obstacle encountered not only in the practice of leadership but in the selection and placement of leaders. It is not especially difficult to find persons who are leaders. It is quite another matter to place these persons in situations where they will be able to function as leaders. It becomes clear that an adequate analysis of leadership involves not only a study of leaders but also of situations.[7]

The dozen essays on leadership in libraries and library organizations were solicited from leaders and/or persons who have had substantive experience in the areas addressed in each essay.

Florence M. Kirwin, in the first essay, explains that the small public library will be competing more and more with the private information sector. The first type of library to deliver services to local clients should be the small public library. Leadership will also focus on organizing small public libraries by function.

"The Warrior/Philosopher: Leadership in the Large Public Library," by Donald J. Sager, predicts that leaders of large public libraries can expect the fight for funds, recognition, participation, and flexibility to become more difficult and to demand greater strength in the future. In addition, it is essential for the leader to maintain a philosophical perspective of emerging library services.

According to Harold G. Lord, the leader of the school library/media program must give particular emphasis to the funding and adapting to new technology. The electronic information age will have a positive impact on the library/media program only if the leader will exercise the necessary initiative and implementation.

Sheryl Anspaugh discusses the effect the community college environment will have on leadership. She notes a correlation between leadership and environmental factors, giving an illustration of how situational conditions affect leadership.

Edward E. Shaw, president of The Research Libraries Group, Inc., describes the general context (i.e., mission and resources) of the research university and its relationship to the library. The use of stategic planning and having the courage to fail are essential ingredients for strong leadership in a research university library.

Advances in telecommunication and computer technologies will inexorably alter the organization and daily life of special libraries. Stephanie H. Stowe sees the special librarian of the future as a generalist, one who will have to use creativity to meet the new challenges.

Michael Gorman describes the leader in technical services as someone who "combines administrative skills (an organized mind) with personal sensitivity (a good heart). S/he must be competent without being mechanistic, must be visionary and idealistic without being wooly-minded, and must be a leader without being power hungry."

The future will find collection development integrally involved with resource sharing and dependent upon electronic access to the resources of other libraries. Dora Biblarz predicts that collections will become far more specialized in the near future.

According to Carolyn Dusenbury, the mission of reference service in the future requires the development of a theory. Formulation of the theory necessitates separating the real issues from the red herrings.

Thomas J. Galvin discusses why the leader of a library school has to be held accountable for its organizational direction, as he describes revitalizing the curriculum, responding to the need for continuing education, and relating to the impact of new technology.

Leadership requirements for state library agencies and state library associations are detailed by the editor. He concludes that it is mandatory for these two groups to develop a symbiotic relationship.

Elizabeth W. Stone, president of the American Library Association, indicates that the executive board of ALA must be concerned with the development of leadership skills, and she advocates leadership in developing unity in ALA and strategic planning as necessary for analyzing the strengths and weaknesses of ALA. Promoting lifelong learning and using new technologies will be ongoing goals for the Association.

REFERENCES

1. James MacGregor Burns, *Leadership* (New York: Harper & Row, 1978), p. 1.

2. Henry Steele Commager, "Our Leadership Crisis: America's Real Malaise," *Los Angeles Times,* Part V (November 11, 1979): 1.

3. Burns, p. 18.

4. Warren Bennis, *The Leaning Ivory Tower* (San Francisco: Jossey-Bass Publishers, 1973), pp. 83–84.

5. Warren G. Bennis, ''Where Have All the Leaders Gone?'' *Technology Review*, 79 (March/April, 1977): 37–46.

6. Bennis, ''Where Have All the Leaders Gone?'', p. 45–46.

7. Ralph M. Stodgill, *Handbook of Leadership* (New York: The Free Press, 1974), p. 64.

Contributors

Sheryl Anspaugh is Director of Libraries, Houston Community College System, Houston, Texas.

Dora Biblarz is Head, Collection and Acquisition Services, Arizona State University, Tempe, Arizona.

Carolyn Dusenbury is Head, Reference Service, Arizona State University, Tempe, Arizona.

Thomas J. Galvin is Dean, School of Library and Information Science, University of Pittsburgh, Pittsburgh, Pennsylvania.

Michael Gorman is Director of Technical Services, University of Illinois, Urbana, Illinois.

Florence M. Kirwin is a doctoral student, School of Library and Information Management, University of Southern California, Los Angeles, California. She has served as Director, Aspen and Pitkin County Library, Aspen, Colorado.

Harold G. Lord is Director of Media Services, Littleton School District, Littleton, Colorado. Under his leadership, the Littleton School District won first place honors in the School Library/Media Program of the Year Award in 1976. The program is sponsored by the Encyclopedia Britannica Companies.

Donald E. Riggs is University Librarian, Arizona State University, Tempe, Arizona. He has served as President of the Colorado Library Association and the West Virginia Library Association.

Donald J. Sager is former Commissioner, Chicago Public Library, Chicago, Illinois. He is President-Elect of the Public Library Association, American Library Association.

Edward E. Shaw is President, The Research Libraries Group, Inc., Stanford, California.

Elizabeth W. Stone is President, American Library Association. She is also Dean, School of Library and Information Science, The Catholic University of America, Washington, D.C.

Stephanie H. Stowe is Library Director, Denver Museum of Natural History, Denver, Colorado.

Diversity and Expanding Choices: Challenges to Leadership in Small Public Libraries

by Florence M. Kirwin

Whatever the exact state of the small public library by the year 2000, it is certain that the role of its administrator will differ fundamentally from the present-day role as s/he attempts to lead the institution in new directions, to deliver new services, and to serve new needs. Administrators will be called upon to do more than manage; they will have to creatively and strongly lead libraries into the future. Some of the activities the future leader will have to perform can be outlined. For example, leaders must creatively plan and manage the direction and destiny of the library; they must interact within the interorganizational network of agencies, government bodies, and constituency groups who will demand attention and accountability; and they must take up the task of identifying new societal trends and values and, thus, shape the direction of the library to meet developing new needs and demands.

FORCES OF CHANGE AFFECTING LIBRARIES

It is not a simple task to characterize the changes and trends that will occur in society and that will have an impact on the nature of the future small public library. No attempt is made here to give a comprehensive survey. However, a number of trends have been identified which will be increasingly important and deserve consideration. The trends are:

1. The burgeoning diversity of information technologies which are working to radically alter the type, structure, and definition of information as it has existed in human history.

2. Widespread change in the nature of the family unit and changes in social values which are causing totally new social and organizational patterns and problems to emerge.
3. A growing skepticism and questioning by large sections of society on the soundness and rightness of the values and goals of community institutions, such as libraries.

DIVERSITY OF THE INFORMATION SECTOR

The first major challenge to libraries is the exploding diversity of newly developing information products. It has been said in jest that, if you thought you were up-to-date on the latest technological advances when you left work on Friday, you will be behind times when you return to work on Monday; advances and developments are occurring that rapidly.

Satellite-based communications will be big business by the year 2000, and the consumer will be able to pull television programming from Nigeria or from the next block of his/her community, depending upon his/her needs and desires. Electronic mail with wide-range applications and systems, such as interactive banking services offered via the consumer's television set, are not far away in the future. The Prestel interactive system in England already offers the consumer a variety of services and information through the home television set.

These new information systems will come into our homes at the same time, whether we live in the city or the suburbs, because the electronic network which will permit these developments is already in place across the country. Rural and less densely populated areas will feel the impact of these new technological possibilities at nearly the same time as the cities. It is significant to mention this fact because, for the first time in history, innovation will be simultaneous. In the past, the diffusion of innovation and technology spread slowly from the major population centers due to the high costs of installation in less densely populated areas.

The development of the private information sector will increasingly compete with the local public library. Private vendors are already moving boldly ahead with the creation of services and the delivery of information to customers for a fee. Private information sources are raising the expectation of the consumer and hence are creating an economic commodity of information. At a more steady state than in the past, consumers will be willing to pay for services which give them easy access to high quality information. The secret of the private vendors' success lies not in their ability to provide more information but in their ability to allow the consumer to get by with less information that is of high quality and timely.

Small public libraries may believe they will escape the impact of the new technologies based on the argument that their small budgets will only permit the purchasing of traditional materials (i.e., books and records). All libraries, large and small, may be directly affected by the information revolution because they may not have a choice. According to a study done by Arthur D. Little, Inc. on the impact of electronic systems on news publishing through 1992, it was noted that those who are able to break away from their traditional roles as newspaper or magazine publishers and become broad-based information providers will find important additional channels for marketing their news and information services.[1] The message for libraries seems clear; libraries may be only one of many outlets for publications and may find themselves forced to accept the choice and trends set by the publishers.

There is yet another form of diversity that is occurring in the information sector that is being promoted by the development of the new technologies. For the first time in history, through the advent of the photocopying machine, the videotape player, and the tape recorder, it is now possible for the consumer/user to break down and also segment information packages (books, journals, records) according to his/her particular needs. We are all familiar with the photocopies of articles and miscellaneous snippets of information which land on our desks at one time or another. Tape recorders, for instance, allow us to record, erase, or change audio material at will. Videotape recorders offer us a similar capability. We can easily create our own form of information or entertainment by changing, altering, lengthening, or shortening the creation of others. Videodiscs will offer more than just the possibility of breaking down packages of information; they will offer the ability to randomize access to what we wish to see. Users will be able to skip around in a disc, rather than being confined to a backward or forward linear progression. All of these developments cannot help but alter the way information providers, producers, and users interact. The whole concept and understanding of the rights of the information's creator, as opposed to the creative, educational needs of the user, will undergo revision. It is possible that the library may be one of the battlegrounds for this conflict, since libraries have traditionally supported copyright rules and restrictions while concurrently championing the right of the user to have full access to the maximum amount of information to meet his/her needs.

SOCIETAL CHANGES

The breakdown of the traditional nuclear family unit is already producing dramatic societal changes. There are increasing numbers of single persons and single-parent households. More individuals are entering the workplace to support themselves and their families. As a consequence, the amount of leisure time individuals have available and the hours when leisure occurs are both changing. It is not a coincidence that California has a high proportion of singles and single-parent households and also has a large number of supermarkets, department stores, and other agencies which stay open late at night or even all night. Banks and other service facilities are developing automated teller services and self-service units to allow clients to serve themselves at times convenient to the client, rather than forcing the client to conform to the facility's schedule.

The family unit revolution also spells the end of the "child-centered" society as it has existed for the past few decades. The character of the population is changing rapidly as fewer births occur and the life span is extended. A dramatic drop in the number of young children and students will have a pronounced impact on all libraries, especially small and rural public libraries, since these institutions have traditionally been committed to serving the educational/informational needs of family units including children and young adults.

A decline in the number of students or children will not be the only significant change by the year 2000. It is well-known that libraries are based on the idea that literacy and education are basic factors of achieving success in life and in one's chosen occupation. Literacy, achieved through reading, has always been the keystone of the educational process. It allows individuals to broaden their horizons, to stimulate their imaginations, and to create personal satisfaction and knowledge. The future may be quite different; it is perceived to be an environment populated by televisions, computers, and intelligent telephones. Individuals will be able to bypass reading as a means of acquiring information and knowledge since they may be able to "picture" the required data or information. For the first time since the development of the printing press, literacy and intelligence may be discounted from one another. Alvin Toffler in the *Third Wave* suggests the alteration of the "info-sphere" cannot help but alter our minds.[2] This will, in turn, alter the way we think about problems, the way we synthesize information to draw conclusions, and the way we engage in other thought processes. The implication is that all of our knowledge about library use and usage patterns of users may shortly be obsolete and useless for planning purposes.

Another trend that is likely to significantly affect small and rural libraries is the upsurging interest in small communities. It is difficult to outline all the reasons why increasing interest in nonurban communities is occurring, but certainly the problems of scarce energy, the high crime problems of the cities, and the social isolation effects of urban areas have helped to spark an interest in living in a smaller, more easily controlled situation. The return to the smaller community has stimulated interest in greater participation in local affairs. That increased participation, in turn, has the potential to cause the politicalization of the library and to cause community special interest groups to put pressure on the local facilities for more specialized services and resources. The role of the professional may be affected and altered as administrative processes and decisions are increasingly subject to legal proceedings brought forth by disgruntled employees and unhappy constituents. Ironically, the increasing interest in small communities may lead to problems of growth and expansion for these communities as more persons seek to live in these areas. Small public libraries in the 90s and beyond may find themselves having to develop means of solving problems of growth without the support of state and federal funds.

INSTITUTIONAL CHANGES

The nature of the small public library as an organization will also likely undergo a transformation by the year 2000. The basic impetus for change will come from a wholesale alteration in the concept of an organization as a "workplace." Information technologies and the impact of scarce energy may cause dramatic changes in the types of activities and work that are performed in the building that is known as a library. Microprocessing and word processing equipment tied to telecommunication lines may mean that book processing, cataloging chores, and even the patron's information inquiry may be handled without a single individual entering a library building. Aiding the altering of the workplace will be the fundamental change that has occurred in the basic formula of organization. There has been a revision in the standard that institutions have operated on for the past decades; the practice has been that of hiring from a pool of inexpensive human labor for the operation of expensive machines. Within the next 20 years, the availability of cheap, personal computers and machines and the rapid growth in labor costs will result in dramatic transformations in the organization.

In conjunction with this line of thinking, Paul Wasserman has already issued a call to the library profession to begin designing library institutions so individuals working in them can be more than replacement parts for the organization.[3] Small public libraries are particularly in need of improving the utilization and organization of personnel in their institutions. Different staffing standards for public libraries have concluded that there should be one professional librarian for every two nonprofessional positions. Empirical evidence would reflect that this standard is largely unmet in many areas today, with the gap growing larger as funding pressures intensify and budget cuts abound. The consequence is the increasing exposure of the public to clerks, technicians, and assistants who have not been trained and whose education has been often ignored or neglected by library professionals.

As we will need greater diversity in the definition of roles of nonprofessionals, we will also need greater variety in the role of professionals. This will be especially true for professionals charged with the administration of our public libraries. It seems that one of the impacts of technological revolution will be to free human beings from the mindless, repetitive routine that has comprised a large part of basic library operation. Individuals freed of this bulk of routine work will be free to perform other functions directly related to service to clients. Further, professionals will be devoting more time to client-related services. This change will result in the redefinition of professional work. Rather than ''professional'' being defined by the task (e.g., reference, cataloging), the future professional may be a professional administrator or a professional information counselor.

As jobs become less specialized and/or repetitive, work may become more satisfying and rewarding. Flexible schedules of working hours are likely to create more acceptable working patterns and, therefore, more satisfaction for employees. It is also possible that, as human labor costs increase, the leadership will try to seek ways to improving work productivity by more creative salary/benefit packages, rather than by offering incremental raises. Perhaps by the year 2000, library employees will be more involved in decisions about the manner in which they are to be compensated for their work, and they will also have active participation in designing their individual benefit packages tailored to their needs. For example, a single individual might choose to have more vacation days per year, a four-day work week, and a tuition remission package. An individual with a family might choose a standard work week with extensive medical and dental coverage.

The nature of the organization may also be affected by changes in the community. Localism and the increasing participation of interested community individuals in decision making will cause an impact on the mission of the library. Basic power struggles may break out as different groups struggle to gain influence or power over the mission of the organization. In smaller communities, libraries frequently serve the needs of a highly diverse group of users due to the absence of a supporting network of bookstores and other information agencies. Library administrators of these smaller libraries may find themselves in highly vulnerable positions, if local citizens begin to seek control or to dictate how libraries should serve the communities. If library leadership does not attempt to define the goals of the library, the community may assume this job itself, excluding professional input or expertise.

LIBRARIES IN THE YEAR 2000

The view presented here of the future small public library is not intended to be comprehensive. A few of the trends that will have an impact on small libraries will be changes in the nature of the governance of the institution, changes in service policies, and changes in the institutional and physical nature of the organization. It is predicted that, based on the direction of current events, the future will include the following:

1. There will be a shift of power away from lay administrative boards toward consolidation of administrative control in the hands of professional library administrators.
2. Small public libraries will be the first (the leaders) in stimulating a new trend toward greater emphasis and creativity in the delivery of services to local clients.
3. Small public libraries will lose much of their separate institutional identity in communities as the adoption of centralized computer information systems and more standardized administrative practices help to collapse the separateness and autonomy in decision making that libraries have enjoyed outside of the control of their jurisdictional units.

The first trend, the decline in the power of the administrative lay board, is occurring as state legislation, such as recently passed in California, downgrades administrative boards to the status of advisory groups. It is projected that, within 20 years, most public libraries, even the smallest, will be led by professional managers. As library education continues to improve its methods of teaching management techniques and, as the entire process of management becomes more complex, centralization of control under a library manager is expected.

The trend toward localism will also affect the nature of decision making in libraries. It has been common in the past for libraries to look to the professional or state standard for guidelines by which to establish and measure services. However, as budget cuts occur and other financial constraints are placed on the library, there must be a new emphasis placed on the local determination of institutional priorities. The 1979 Conference of the International City Management Association has already recognized this trend, by calling for ''greater skepticism about the value of central government grants . . . to [be] exerted by local governments. . . . Buying back independence may mean doing without . . . .''[4]

Small public libraries may be able to create a more integrated position of power in their communities. Adoption of community analysis techniques for assessing local needs or implementation of a planning process for public libraries can be mechanisms for small libraries to study their communities and their status within them. Libraries as information agencies are in the unique position of serving as centralized collection and dissemination points of necessary data and information about the local community. Librarians may have new roles as counselors, educators, and expert witnesses to lay committees and boards who seek knowledge and information about the community for planning and decision purposes.

Implementation of computerized budgetary and accounting information systems will draw the library under greater control of its jurisdictional unit. Local libraries will consider themselves, or will be considered, departments of the jurisdictional unit, rather than autonomous institutions which are separately governed and administered. An example of the effect of information control enhancing the power of those who control it can be seen in the change in university governance patterns which began occurring during the past few years. Information systems for budgeting, accounting, and student records were developed and implemented which have fundamentally altered the balance of power of decision making in these institutions. Administrators can now control figures and quantitative outcomes of the organization, rather than assessing performance on the basis of academic values and priorities as debated by the faculty.[5]

A change in the autonomy of the library will likely force libraries to reevaluate a number of their fundamental tenets. There may be an increasing challenge to redefine the notion of providing universal access and opportunity of use to all clients with the idea of the need for a cost-benefit ratio of operations. Cost-benefit ratio simply means that any action or direction of the institution must produce results equal to or greater than its expense, a clear challenge to the idea of free, unlimited access. City management is already grappling with the problem. According to Agnes Griffen, local government must begin to regulate the demand for both government services and public goods in general through use of pricing mechanisms and through employment of marketing techniques that reduce demand. Basic or essential levels of services may be paid out of general revenue, but nonessential levels of usage may also have a price.[6]

Small public libraries will be the first to discover they are unable to operate as self-supporting institutions and, thus, they are likely to move toward charging for services which can be supported by no other means. However, small libraries may also be able to develop diversified fund-raising activities in their local communities to supplement budget revenues. In this manner, small libraries may reach a new compromise between two principles: libraries can provide access to certain basic resources and services while, at the same time, charging fees for certain services tailored to fulfill individual needs.

SOCIAL ISSUES

The future small public library may be profoundly different from present-day libraries in the way its role in relation to basic social issues is interpreted. Small libraries generally have a close relationship with their clients; they are not like the anonymous, bureaucratic structures of the cities. Librarians and clients are likely to interact with one another in a variety of roles in the community which promote shared interests and values. Small libraries are also more likely to recognize that there are limited alternative sources of information available to their clients and that both access and privacy of inquiry are essential components of the provision of quality library service.

I believe that small public libraries will become less neutral about their role as providers of information in three areas which fundamentally affect the ability of individuals to access information. These are the areas of censorship, copyright versus individual use, and privacy of inquiry. It is possible to speculate that small libraries may assume greater advocacy roles in these areas. Advocacy, in this case, is defined as assuming a position as champion of the client's needs and rights and as working to satisfy those needs and secure those rights for the client. The blueprint for adopting this type of service attitude is already available in many libraries which support and run information and referral centers for their communities.[7]

Very little will be expressed in this essay about the issue of censorship except to observe that, as individuals become more involved in localism, they will seek to exercise greater control over their environment and communities. This may, in turn, lead to more emphasis on controlling the types of materials and information which they find harmful or inconsistent with those environments. It seems reasonable to assume that censorship of materials will continue to occur with more frequency. Small libraries will be forced to take a stand in order to protect their rights to provide and deliver materials needed in their communities. Local librarians may have to defend their selection policies more publicly and more vigorously in the face of intensifying conservative community opinions and growing constituent diversity. If librarians expect to lead communities to accept their decisions regarding the design and provision of information resources and services, they cannot passively follow community dictums which would limit access to information.

The second area where advocacy and leadership are needed is in safeguarding the consumer's right to manipulate information packages (namely books, periodicals, records) according to the demands of personal need. I do not wish to take issue with the basic right of the creator and author to be paid royalties or the right of the publisher to collect reasonable fees for use of materials. I am suggesting that the trend of development of various information technologies will put the librarian squarely between the rights of the information producer and the rights of the user to use that information. In the past years, libraries and librarians have chosen to support the information producers in our willingness to understand and uphold copyright restrictions concerning limited copying and reproduction of printed, visual, and audio materials. The development of new technologies, the rising cost of purchase rates, and the increasing need of individuals for quality information will challenge librarians to make a choice between the needs of the supplier or producer and the priorities and needs of users. I believe librarian leaders will have to take a stand. They will have to challenge some of the more unreasonable copyright restrictions, such as those that apply to journal copying for reserve purposes; they will have to be prepared to understand and to influence copyright legislation; and they will have to educate the public regarding their positions and philosophies on these issues.

A third social policy where leadership is important is the privacy of inquiry. We are living in a society that places more and more value on the acquisition of information which can be used to increase our career and personal goals. It is often desirable that the seeking of this information be confidential since the information itself can be indicative of the nature of the problems or intentions. Yet, the right of the individual to seek personal and "life-style" information privately has barely been raised as an issue in library literature. Patrons may increasingly be forced to request desired materials via paperwork procedures, such as interlibrary loan forms, computer inquiry assistance forms, and other nonprivate means. One of the exciting and little recognized roles for the small public library may be to collect and maintain materials which the client can utilize with the maximum protection from supervision. The professional librarian may also have to develop and promote the concept of libraries as sources of protected and private inquiring centers.

SERVICES

The small public library of the future will likely experience profound changes in the physical configuration of its facility and in the nature of its operation. Energy costs, the heavy emphasis on people-oriented services, and the rising costs of human labor may all contribute to make the library less visible as a physical facility in the community. The brick Carnegie building which dominates the block is clearly passé. Small community libraries will have to seek means to free every dollar of their budgets to provide services and to purchase materials. They may be forced to give up their fixed locations. Store-front libraries, libraries in rental quarters, and libraries in multipurpose community facilities will be the trend of the future.

At the same time, technology will allow public libraries to move ahead to develop innovative and creative methods of delivering services and resources to their clienteles. The development of microprocessors and home computers opens the door to computer applications in all phases of library operations. Small libraries will be wise to concentrate their energy and attention on developing means of improving services to their clients. Within the next decade, it is hoped that the organization and access problems of computerization involving bibliographic citations, computer search strategies, and AACR2 conversions will be recognized to be more of a primary concern for the large public and research library, while the small public library will focus on user education and information about the new possibilities available for accessing information.

Much of the new information technology will be financially available to small public libraries. By the year 2000, it is probable that many self-service mechanisms will be developed which will free human labor from many of the housekeeping tasks. Within 20 years, there will be self-service circulation checkout stations. Future libraries may have drive-up windows which would permit them to operate during slow periods with minimum staffing. Certainly, this type of solution would be effective for staffing libraries late at night or during specific weekend hours. It is also conceivable that libraries of the future will have services whereby users could transmit videotaped messages over cable to other similar systems. The library would receive the request, locate the desired material or information, and transmit the item to the patron without either the patron or the librarian moving from their respective locations.

LEADERSHIP FOR THE YEAR 2000

What kind of person will be needed to run the small public library in the year 2000? For an answer, consider the following statements made by Chinese philosopher Lao Tse on the nature of leadership:

The leader is best
When people barely know he exists.
Not so good when people obey and acclaim him,
Worse when they despise him.
Fail to honor people, they fail to honor you.
But of a good leader, who talks little,
When his work is done, his aim fulfilled, they will say,
'We did this ourselves.'[8]

If we seek to reject the idea of the librarian as merely a manager who reacts to events and we strive to create viable libraries operated by professional leaders, then we must pay heed to Lao Tse's words. Leaders must lead and not just manage the resources effectively for the given task at hand. Leadership is the delicate balance between authoritarianism on the one hand and the danger of aimlessness or drift on the other. Leadership at the level of the small public library will require individuals who have a number of qualities including the agility of a dancer, the mind of a politician, and the determination of a bull. The small library will be dependent on the skills and abilities of its leaders to design innovative solutions to meet the turbulent and uncertain environment of the future. The leaders will undertake the difficult task of redefining and redirecting outmoded ideas and patterns into new organizational directions and imperatives.

The first job involving the introduction of new leadership patterns to libraries is to rethink the function of leadership in the organizational context. Traditionally, leadership has been characterized as the exercise of control over the institution and as a set of behaviors which stimulated worker motivation.

Leadership has been analyzed from the perspective of the organizational principles of hierarchy of levels and the existence of job differentiation. Traditional leadership has been concerned with giving structure to an organization in order to promote stable organizational activities and a reliable outcome product. To achieve this, organizations have had jobs which are organized in hierarchical fashion so that upper levels enforce and supervise the activities of the lower levels in the production of their work. Each individual has a specialized and differentiated task which produces a repetitive and, therefore, reliable product which can be observed and controlled for quality. Persons become specialized within jobs as the result of differentiation, and the job of the traditional leader is to coordinate and weave together the different specialized areas into a functioning organization. In libraries, there are reference librarians who are independent in their job tasks from those of technical services librarians or children's services librarians. Administrators are concerned with supervising the activities of these different units and coordinating their activities.

The traditional model of leadership has been concerned with control of worker activities, as well as with coordination, leaving little time for other tasks. If we are to have leaders who have time for the necessary future leadership activities, such as interaction with the community and planning activities, then we must reject the traditional leadership model and seek a new one.

The future leadership model would be based on a restructuring of the organization of activities in libraries. Rather than maintain a hierarchical structure with specialized and differentiated jobs, work would be organized into large units or functions. Individuals would be part of a group which would have responsibility for all activities associated with their particular functions. They would also share responsibility for the performance of tasks and would control the quality of the output. Jobs would not be highly structured, nor would division of labor be important. Professionals, technicians, and clerks would be members of a group. For example, one group would be responsible for the informational service activities of the library. The group would perform and control cataloging details and specialized record keeping, as well as the planning and design of services offered in the small public library. Another group would be responsible for the educational function or mission by creating adult and children's programs and by designing innovative educational packaging and display of materials.

Reorganization by function would provide greater connection between the goals of the library—to serve the recreational, educational, and informational needs of the citizenry—and the strategy and activities necessary to reach those goals. Work group reorganization would also produce measurable outcomes from each unit which could be observed and which could be compared with the stated goals of the organization.

The impact on leadership would be to free managers and administrators from much of the supervision and control activities that have been traditionally part of the administrative routine. Administrators would have time to think and to plan library activities, in other words, to lead, rather than to merely react to trends and events. Conceivably, the library leader might attempt to manipulate the environment in which the library operates. Manipulation would involve the leader in not only participating in community decision processes but also in seeking to influence political activity, in seeking means to influence legislation and social policy affecting user needs, and in engaging in assertive and active public relations activities to educate and influence public opinion about the value of library activities.

Based on the idea of a new style of leadership, it is possible to outline the following four new types of library leader styles which might emerge:

The judicial librarian leader. The librarian would serve as the judge between two sets of imperatives. The institutional imperatives are the constraints and requirements within which the institution seeks to operate. Examples of institutional imperatives are strategies to reduce operating costs of the physical facility or methods to increase longevity of use of materials by reducing wear and imposing fines for loss or abuse. The second set of imperatives are user-oriented and represent the needs and demands of the institution's client group. User imperatives emphasize the needs of the users and would stress specialized collection development or making full use of resources for collection building. Pressure to provide more hours of service and more branch facilities would be other examples of user imperatives.

The judicial role would involve leadership to narrow the range of choices and priorities. The decision process should create greater certainty about the nature of the library's role by eliminating conflicting and competing alternatives. Librarians may have to understand and apply principles of ''social justice'' which support the idea that there are baseline services which must be offered to certain groups, no matter the cost or the conflicting demands of other constituent groups. The right of access for the elderly and handicapped to library facilities are examples of basic rights.

The mediator/designer librarian leader. While the judicial leader would eliminate possibilities based on constraints, the mediating leader would involve the creative and delicate task of designing unique services and resources to meet the demands of local priorities and needs. The approach would be to first evaluate the possibilities of services, to select several of the best possible approaches, and to choose and design specialized services and programs.

This leadership activity would involve the knowledge and use of technology and social/behavior theory and research as the tools of the design process. Such leadership style would also demand that the librarian be knowledgeable concerning information transfer processes among different groups in the community and have an understanding of the structure of knowledge that would be most useful to these groups.

As mediator, activities of the leader would involve contact with groups inside and outside of the institution. The mediator would operate external to the library, working with advisory and special interest groups, community planning groups, and government officials. There is some evidence that this external mediator role is already emerging. A recent *Library Journal* article, ''The Invisible Director: The Emerging Metropolitan Library Executive,'' indicates library administrators may be spending only 15 percent of their time on internal administration and 85 percent lobbying, speaking in public, negotiating budgets, and resolving legal matters.[9]

Although it was predicted earlier that administrative boards will very likely disappear as governing bodies, the mediating leader may consider the creation of lay advisory groups whose function would be that of helping the local community environment.

Decision makers will be forced to make decisions about directions of services and resources with less and less assurance that the choices they are making will be the correct ones, due to the diversity of choice and the rapidly changing environment. The librarian must take the lead in analyzing and evaluating services, resources, institutional and administrative performance, and overall effectiveness. Advisory groups can perform important functions in the collection and analysis of information to make inferences and guesses about the best course of future development. In fancy language, this is the process of forecasting for the future. Advisory groups could have vital roles in information processing in order to assist management in making decisions.

There is an internal mediator role also involving the negotiation of differences between role performances and expectations of organizational individuals and groups. The mediator would maintain the job of coordinating and balancing the different work group or unit functions. Mediators may develop differential pay scales or reward systems based on how valuable the service or the individual is to the organization. Value might be based on external measurement. It is conceivable that community users may ultimately have a role, or some influence, in judging a public employee's worth and value in relation to a perception of the amount and value of the service the user receives from that individual.

The collegial librarian leader. The role of this leader is based on professional knowledge and competence. Allegiance is to the professional knowledge base, the ethics of librarianship, and belief in the highest standards of scholarship and education. A genuine concern for the quality of services and resources offered by the library would be part of this role.

These leaders would have a personal commitment to engage in continuing education for themselves, as well as to help all members of the organization to improve their education and skills. Leaders in libraries must demand custom-tailored education products from educational, governmental, and professional organizations and agencies. Leaders must challenge educational institutions to deliver their products in the local community, rather than forcing individuals to travel to the university or college. Also, an important task of the collegial library leader would be to insist that research and educational institutions provide support and assistance for helping practitioners solve their problems. An emphasis on incorporating experimental and laboratory programs as part of library education may help close the gap between the theory of library education and the concerns of library practice.

The nurturing librarian leader. This is not the charismatic leader concerned with leading workers and motivating them. This leader would be concerned with structuring the library workplace and institution to allow for the greatest satisfaction of organizational participants despite limited resources and budgetary funds. The nurturing leader is creative and operates as more than the simple ''provider'' who assembles the necessary resources. Nurturing leadership will stimulate the development of creativity and even help individuals to renew or transform themselves, depending upon their needs. Transformation is the process of the renewal of energy and the refocusing of talents and skills. Nurturing leaders will also have greater concern for the relation between life-style commitments and the work-life requirements of the staff. Nurturing implies a high tolerance for ''nonconformity'' by individuals from the established procedures/traditions. Nurturing leaders will definitely be required to have qualities of idealism, flexibility, and sensitivity if they are to be effective in the process of helping individuals to achieve self-actualization in our library institutions.

CONCLUSION

In conclusion, the future of the small public libraries will be affected and influenced by many of the impacts felt by larger public libraries. Small institutions will be forced to cope with new societal demands and new technological developments at the same time that large institutions will be struggling to adapt. There will be no compendium of wisdom or recounting of practical experience to guide large or small libraries. How well the small public library fares in the post-industrial society of the future will be highly dependent upon the type and quality of leadership which emerges in this small institution. If librarians at the local level seek to lead, adapt, and redesign the traditional institution, then small public libraries have a bright future. Failure to accept the challenge can only result in the gradual withering and diminishing importance of these libraries. Time will tell.

REFERENCES

1. ''Home TV Centers to Upset Print Media in 1990's,'' *Editor and Publisher* 118 (February 24, 1979): 9.

2. Alvin Toffler, *The Third Wave* (New York: Bantam, 1980), p. 537.

3. Paul Wasserman, *The New Librarianship: A Challenge for Change* (New York: Bowker, 1972), p. 287.

4. Agnes Griffen, ''Report to PLA on the International City Management Association Conference, 1979,'' *Public Libraries* 19 (1980): 27–28.

5. Jeffrey Pfeffer, *Organizational Design* (Arlington Heights, IL: AHM Publishing, 1978), p. 256.

6. Griffen, pp. 27–28.

7. Clara S. Jones, *Public Library Information and Referral Service* (Syracuse, NY: Gaylord Bros., 1978), p. 265.

8. Whitter Bynner, *The Way of Life According to Lao Tse* (New York: John Day Co., 1944), p. 34.

9. James Baughman, ''The Invisible Director: The Emerging Metropolitan Library Executive,'' *Library Journal* 105 (June 15, 1980): 1357–61.

The Warrior/Philosopher: Leadership in the Large Public Library

by Donald J. Sager

The condition of the nation's larger city libraries forecasts the condition of their cities in the years to come. Deteriorated, understaffed, heavily used, and nearing bankruptcy, these institutions are the first victims of the cities' budget problems. Library administrators and board members often find themselves conducting a form of guerrilla warfare in an effort to preserve and, if at all possible, to advance the goals to which their institutions are dedicated.

There is no prescriptive solution to the above circumstances. Many large public libraries have gone through decades of growth and are now facing the bleak reality of retrenchment. The administration of these larger public libraries can only seek new philosophies based on insight to community needs and current trends to guide them in their responsibilities in the coming decades. The traditional solutions can no longer be applied. Postponement until next year's budget process is not the answer, for next year will only be worse. The library's director must reform the institution's services; gain maximum use of personnel, facilities, and appropriation; and creatively coax or force the library to respond to the insatiable demands of a clientele less and less willing or able to support the status quo. Maintenance or preservation of existing levels of services with declining resources is not sufficient. The larger public library must evolve or disappear.

LEADERSHIP DEFINED

Defining leadership under these circumstances represents an interesting challenge. One of the most commonly accepted definitions states that leadership is the process of making things happen.[1] Most library administrators I know would agree with that, but many would also add that what is happening is not always caused by them and is not necessarily for the best. I have been told that today it is impossible to provide leadership in a larger public library; one is simply carried along by the sheer momentum of the daily crises created by decades of neglect and bad decisions, almost like being on the crest of an avalanche.

I happen to disagree with that perception (on the basis of my personal philosophy and not scientific study). There is a theory known as path/goal that defines the leader as a person who clarifies goals and removes barriers.[2] I want to develop that view of leadership in this essay, for I believe it can provide some guidance in a land where there are no road maps and no prior precedents. I want to review some strategies for leadership for both the present and future. The administrator of the larger public library today must be a philosopher in clarifying and restating the goals of his/her institution and must have the savvy to use all available resources to fight for those ends.

GOALS AND POLICIES

We have gone through an era when heavy emphasis was placed on the broadest possible participation in goal setting for an institution. Administrators were taught techniques in gaining staff input. Federal policy decreed that users and citizens should be involved in the development of services, and this was soon a policy adhered to by all governmental units. Our first White House Conference on Libraries and Information Science was designed to include users and citizens as a majority of the delegates in the development of new goals for libraries.

The result of this policy has been a curious inertia. By and large, the public and the staff are usually satisfied with either the same services, or a greater investment in those services, rather than any new insight or demand for a dynamic new approach to the delivery of library service. An analysis of the recommendations of the White House Conference yields an array of glittering generalities which have simply supported programs such as interlibrary cooperation. All have long been accepted as part of library development. The conclusion of the conference was that more of the same is needed. Unfortunately, those recommendations arrived concurrently with a vast wave of retrenchment at the federal, state, and local levels which will assure that less of the same will result.

The development of goals by consensus may be a necessary step for acceptance, but it neither represents leadership nor provides a philosophical basis for the survival of the urban public library. Creativity is a rare commodity, and enlarging participation in goal setting will not improve the likelihood of finding creative solutions to the problems of urban libraries. Leadership has to assume the responsibility for forming creative goals that will satisfy as many of the needs that leadership perceives are fundamental and necessary to the institution.

Just as committees are more efficient in responding to clearly stated problems, staff are more effective in the conversion of clear goals to practical objectives. The administrator of any large urban library today will learn that if s/he relies upon his/her staff for the answers to the problems faced by that institution, the answers will be more staff, more materials, and better facilities. It falls upon the effective leader to propose goals that will lead to solutions to the problems the institution faces and then to gain the participation of the staff in modification of those goals and in designing the objectives and techniques to achieve them. The administrator who fails to offer goals which provide solutions to the library's problems is not demonstrating leadership but, in fact, is only responding to circumstances and is riding the crest of the avalanche.

In effective leadership, things happen when solutions are proposed and are accepted by those who will have to implement those solutions, as well as by those who must use the services of the institution and pay for those services. The major barrier in dealing with problems, such as inadequate financing, is institutional inertia. The surest means of combating inertia is to change the goals of an institution, and, while that raises other obstacles, it is not the role of a leader to maintain the status quo. By definition, the leader is someone who changes things. I have known many administrators who have the capacity to efficiently manage the operations of a library, ensuring good morale and public satisfaction with the service. But that is not the same thing as leadership, which seeks to alter that institution so that it can better use its resources to meet the needs of the future.

LARGE PUBLIC LIBRARY CHARACTERISTICS

There are some unique aspects of leadership in a large public library. The administrator finds a large budget which holds the opportunity for dramatic services and new methods. The board of directors of a typical large city library is usually amply supplied with those persons who can wield influence necessary to effect change, leaders accustomed to taking steps to ensure that things happen. The staff of a typical urban library is rich in number and in specializations; these human resources can be marshalled. The facilities of a major public library system are awesome, and they form the backbone of the city's cultural and intellectual life.

The typical large city holds celebrities, successful business persons, political leaders, individuals with power and national stature, many of whom owe a debt of gratitude to the library for what it has given them (e.g., Nobel and Pulitzer prize millionaires, and the elite that form the decisions that influence our society). These persons can be called upon to promote the library, to contribute to its collections, and to aid in its operations. The administrator who is not moved by present opportunities is surely dead and does not know it. Leadership should sense these great resources and employ them creatively to solve the problems they face.

Great though these resources may be, their very nature may make them liabilities. The size of the library's budget makes it a target for cuts if other city services are considered more essential. While the library's budget may seem great, the burdens imposed upon its revenues are so immense that realignment or reallocation may seem impossible. Budget size does not guarantee flexibility. Politics may exist in any library system, but they are awesome in the larger city where every constituency struggles to protect the status quo and everything is in delicate balance. The staff that seemed so impressive in terms of numbers and talent vanishes in the cold reality of scheduling demands. There are barely sufficient staff to keep the doors open, and reassignment for new initiatives by the administration is unthinkable and an exercise in futility.

Those grand buildings which may be architectural landmarks turn into horrible white elephants sucking up millions of limited revenues in utility costs and maintenance. They are almost always in the wrong location, proudly centered amid now vacant tenements or land cleared for urban development which has never materialized. The tremendous resources represented by the community turn into hordes of messianic organizations prepared to picket and demand the resignation of the administrator at the least hint of change affecting their turf. Community leadership vanishes each night to the suburbs, leaving the heart of the city as empty as a cemetery on Halloween. Crime threatens staff and public alike, turning outreach into a kamikaze mission.

BUREAUCRACY

Bureaucracy is perhaps the greatest barrier to leadership in a larger city. It is smothering, and, until it is mastered, an administrator is likely to be powerless. There are only two ways to deal with it. Either employ someone who is part of the system and who has grown up with it, and delegate authority to him/her to cope with it, or learn the system yourself, quickly. Coupled with that is the necessity to adjust for the time that it requires for things to happen. One of the qualities of leadership has to be an acute sense of timing. There is always only one time to present a project, and that is the time when it can gain all the necessary approvals. An effective leader must also have an appreciation of the time required for the completion of a project. Leadership is knowing when to apply pressure, and that is only when it will have meaningful impact. If you press for a project during the normal time lag required for everything in a large city, you will be ignored because of your ignorance of the system. If you apply the pressure after the project has languished for months beyond its normal cycle, the project will be ignored because you are obviously too stupid and have too little clout to influence the processing of the project. Otherwise, you would have applied pressure earlier. Determining the right time to exercise your influence, and upon whom, is critical to leadership and essential in a large bureaucracy.

It is certainly true that smaller cities have bureaucracies, and leadership must deal with them. But, in a large city, bureaucracy is a living, breathing animal that sits hugely on its out-basket, blocking everything. Coping with it is both a dark science and an occult art, governed by the city procedures and monitored by the civil service commission, leavened by the increasingly aggressive dictates of multiple jurisdictions of white and blue collar unions. When the staff represented by the Teamsters says they will not work on the day you planned to have the mayor dedicate a new branch library, the mayor will simply have to adjust his/her schedule to the convenience of the Teamsters. It is simply not negotiable.

Mastering the bureaucracy sufficiently to get things done, and avoiding the tendency to succumb to it, is a form of leadership in a large city. It is a humble achievement, and one which is not likely to appear amid the honors in your biography in *Who's Who*, but it is recognized as a symbol of your effectiveness by your colleagues who reap the benefits.

Probably one of the major aspects of leadership is the ability to alter the image of the library in the city. When it is realized that generations of the public and staff have one consistent concept of what the library does and that this has been reinforced by the media, as well as by the public service policies of the institution, by the design of the library's facilities, and even by the engravings on the walls of the building, tampering with that image seems not only foolhardy but downright reckless.

LIBRARY USERS

The predominant image of the American public library is as a supplier of popular fiction and a place for students to complete their homework assignments. Yet, the typical large urban public library is not circulating popular fiction to housewives (or anyone else) with time to kill anywhere near the level it did in the 30s. More than half of those housewives are pursuing careers and have major responsibilities other than the home. Recreation may still seem a legitimate function for the public library, but people have infinitely more ways to recreate today. Students still come in large numbers to do their homework in public libraries (and to vandalize books and reading room tables). But, they also have increasingly well-supplied media centers, access to community college and university libraries, and paperback books, and some of them even take advantage of their new home computers to tap cheap databases.

The American public library is not the place where the majority of Americans go to seek information. They are turning to other alternatives. The problem of the American public library, and especially the large public library, is its image. It has succeeded so well in its initial mission and function that this image seems permanently burned into the consciousness of the public, public officials, library governance, and even the staff.

No administrator will deny that the circulation of popular materials and general reader's advisory assistance is important. However, this is a declining service, an activity that is nearing the end of its life cycle, and the public is less and less willing to support its increasingly high unit cost. We must identify new services and develop our ability to efficiently provide them. It was Peter Drucker who wrote that it is the responsibility of leadership to delegate responsibility for today and to assume responsibility for tomorrow.[3] That is not easy for most administrators, for most of them gained their positions because of their skills in building the collections and services which are currently in use. They have a stake in those resources; their blood and sweat went into painstakingly creating them during times when there were always other priorities. Due to their astute planning, the public is able to obtain the services it needs now. But what about tomorrow's generation?

Even if the administrator has that realization and can read in the statistics what the trends are, there is another barrier which must be surmounted. No one has a clear vision of what those future needs will be. There is virtually no research and development program supported by any major public library today. Even if the funds were available, no one knows how to undertake this type of research reliably or where to begin.

RISK TAKING

Leadership has to invest in tomorrow's breadwinners, and that requires a great deal of courage in changing both the image of the institution and in paring services which, while most will acknowledge as essential today, will not be essential tomorrow. The risk is that the administrator will have an imperfect vision of what the future of that institution should be and will fail in selecting the resources and services to develop in anticipation of future demands.

In automation, the one thing to avoid is being an Alpha site, the first place in which an application or hardware is installed. Everything that can go wrong will happen there, at great expense, delay, public dissatisfaction, and staff frustration. Yet, the leaders in the library profession today are those individuals who risk being an Alpha site; on their experience, we grow. The first break with tradition, whether it is in automation, outreach, home delivery of services, or the development of new types of resources, represents an essential step in the evolution of this venerable institution. There will be mistakes. Leadership is built upon the bedrock of mistakes. If there is anything that haunts the administrator of the large public library, it is the fear of making mistakes. Financially, politically, and administratively, s/he cannot afford it.

POLITICS AND PUBLIC RELATIONS

Nonetheless, the mark of leadership in a large public library is the impact that the administrator has in altering the public's image of the institution. That can be managed in several ways, but the most common strategy is through an effective publicity program. The chief public relations officer for any major public library is its chief executive. While the operation of the library's publicity program can be delegated, it is the chief executive who must establish the tone and the goals. S/he must also make certain that the staff conveys the message in a manner which will alter negative perceptions of the library and build awareness of the direction in which the institution is heading.

Certainly, this is a shared responsibility between the executive, the board, and the staff. But, when all is said and done, the administrator must provide the continuity, the initiative, and the will to see that publicity conveys an image of the institution that is dynamic, responsive to the city's needs, and efficient in the use of available resources. That can only be built by starting at the top, by meeting with the leadership of the local media (both electronic and print) and by communicating to them the goals and objectives of the library. I know of few successful library leaders who do not have a close relationship with the editors and editorial boards of their local major newspapers and the managers and executives of the leading radio and television stations.

In any large city, public relations is often coordinated with the office of the mayor, and good leadership involves the mayor in the major events and announcements of the library. This not only shares the credit for any accomplishments with the mayor, but it also ensures broader coverage of those accomplishments. And, of course, it familiarizes the mayor personally with what improvements and changes the library is undertaking. This has a beneficial impact upon the library's image in a more subtle fashion. The mayor of any city is its most powerful and influential leader, and the mayor's association with the library bestows upon that institution and its administration a portion of that power and leadership. A library and its administration that lacks the support and involvement of its mayor in its activities and goals is going to experience difficulty in altering its image and exercising any leadership.

There is often a reluctance on the part of library governance and its administration to involve the political leadership of the community in library activities. Traditionally, the library is supposed to be above politics, and, certainly, there are valid dangers. No one wants to see the library become a dump for patronage, nor should the administration of the institution change with every election. Yet, the library must work effectively with city hall to see that its goals become part of the mayor's goals and that the mayor's goals are reflected in an appropiate manner by the library. The image should be one of cooperation and teamwork with the mayor and his/her staff.

COMMUNITY DYNAMICS

There is also the grassroots image that must be considered. The typical large city is not homogeneous in the slightest degree. It is composed of ruggedly individualistic neighborhoods bound together by only a common street numbering system. To an outsider, a resident may be a Chicagoan, but, to another Chicagoan, that same individual will really explain that s/he is from Bridgeport, or Edgebrook, or Hyde Park, or any of the other 90 neighborhoods which have been created by ethnic or physical barriers over the city's history. Any large city today is only a collection of neighborhoods, and that understanding is essential to the exercise of leadership.

Once that is realized, the next step is an understanding of the dynamics of community organization. It was Saul Alinsky, the radical organizer who grew up in Chicago, who created the classic methodology for neighborhood improvement. He believed that the best way to mobilize the community, and to hold it together, was to have an opponent who was trying to take something away from the community or perform some action that was threatening to the community. That is a tactic that is almost universal today. Neighborhood groups are created and maintained for only one reason, and that is for confrontation. If the library is to demonstrate leadership and improve its image at the grassroots, that fact has to be realized, and the library's administration must have a community relations program that keeps its ear to the ground.

Many libraries employ a variety of innocent euphemisms for their community relations staff members. In some libraries they are called urban relations specialists. In others, they might be neighborhood outreach workers. Whatever their name, they invariably live in the neighborhood where they work. They are politically involved and street-smart. Their important function is communication, but they are not publicists. The library wants to carry any unpleasant news to the community first, before it goes through the rumor mill. It is hoped that can be avoided. The library administration uses its community relations staff best when it tests the impact of any changes in goals or services upon them and develops strategies for that change with the members of this staff.

In a large city, the closing or consolidation of branches is always a consideration when budgets are reduced and when reallocation of limited funds is required to undertake new initiatives. No community ever wants to see its local library branch closed, even when that facility is unused. It is a situation tailormade for confrontation, and many libraries simply ruin their position of leadership and their image by pitting themselves against neighborhood power structures. In many instances, they also ruin their position and image with the city's administration by passing the buck for these reductions or closings from the community to city hall.

Good community relations require the library administration to find a solution which avoids confrontation at the grassroots and protects the city's administration. It is no easy task, and it requires creativity and patience, as well as sensitivity to the fears and concerns of the community. There is only one strategy to use. Somehow, the community must be brought to the point where they confront the problem and not the library.

STAFF RELATIONS

Staff attitude and morale are critical elements in maintaining the library's image and leadership. There are some administrators who have the personal charisma to instill support, even in the darkest times, despite increasing workloads, increasingly more unpleasant and unsafe working conditions, and inadequate adjustments in pay. But, most administrators are not that fortunate. They have to work for, and earn, the support and respect of their staff. In a large library, that is very tough because the typical administrator is insulated by layers of supervisors; it might be years before s/he is able to meet individually the personnel who deal daily with the public, those library personnel who either create an image of sloth and inefficiency or of dedication and competence.

Like the Wizard of Oz, the administration of a larger library communicates with thunderbolts delivered in the form of memoranda and appears only in the form of his/her aides at the meetings of the staff. There are many strategies which an administrator can employ to establish leadership among the staff, but the most effective is through personal access. The administrator who insulates him/herself from any employee who has a personal grievance with the institution is not exercising leadership and will establish only a reputation of callousness. Conversely, the administrator who continually by-passes supervisors or who devotes all of his/her working day to the individual problems of the staff is not going to get things done. Achieving a balance between access and efficiency is the mark of leadership.

One of the most effective ways of improving morale is to strive for meaningful change in services and resources and to ensure that staff who are participating in that change are aware of the significant contribution that change will have upon the institution and its services to the community. Those staff members also have to receive credit for these contributions. Testing new techniques and the impact of new resources and gaining the advice of the staff who have been involved in that innovation provides greater work satisfaction. Leadership in developing innovative services, experimenting with new types of facilities, and trying variation in policy and procedure will change staff attitude about their work and their philosophy of service, provided that these changes are not being made for the sake of change itself.

FUNDING

Leadership manifests itself most in the funding and budgeting process. While some library administrators will argue that they can do little to influence the amount of revenues their institutions receive, since this is in the hands of the mayor and the city council, it is always aggressive leadership that makes the difference. This process starts in mastering the internal expenses of the institution first. Before any director can seek additional fundings, s/he must be certain that the library is using every available dime and that waste and duplication have been eliminated to the best of everyone's ability.

To exercise any influence in the budgeting process, the administrator must know that his/her own house is in order. Such does not imply a once-a-year sweep through the operations of the institution. It requires a continuing analysis of the system's procedures, coupled with some incentives whenever an employee develops a method to improve productivity or cut costs. Good leadership should find some way to reward those individual improvements, preferably financially. All too often, the employee who finds a better way to accomplish something ends up with little recognition and a great deal more work.

Even though one of the best resources for additional funding can be found in the fat resident in the library's present budget, it must be coupled with the search for alternate sources of income. In the present inflation, the library has to at least double its income every 10 years just to remain at the same level of staffing and materials purchasing. Few manage to achieve that, and the failure is most frequently due to a lack of imagination. Existing sources of revenue (most frequently, property taxes) are typically the only sources considered and, given the attitude of the times, there is almost universal reluctance to increasing them.

As a unique public service, the public library should be eligible for some unique considerations in sources of revenue, and these should be explored with the library's governance and municipal officials. Anything that will give the library a separate income supplemented by the property tax should be considered. Obtaining diversification in income, both by type and tax source, is something in which the library administrator must demonstrate initiative. Generally, that is a responsibility that falls on the shoulders of the municipal finance department.

Most urban libraries today draw support from more than local taxes. Many receive some state and federal support which increasingly supplement local revenues. That is frequently considered soft funding, and, often, it is not even tightly budgeted for fear that the institution may come to rely upon it. Yet, if the public library is ever going to establish a concept of joint support or partnership in sharing the cost of delivering library service to the community, its administration will have to exercise greater leadership in committing those federal and state dollars to specific services to ensure that they are not lost. It is widely recognized that public school system should be supported by a combination of local, state, and federal dollars, and there are similar parallels in the systems of transportation, the environment, and even the arts. There is no reason why libraries cannot gain greater stability through a similar partnership.

With some exceptions, libraries have also failed to demonstrate much initiative in the search for funds from private sources. At this writing, I know of only four major urban public libraries that have full-time professional financial development offices, and most of them are fairly new. As tax-supported institutions, the administrators and boards may believe that it is inappropriate to approach the private sector for additional funding or that it will somehow determine their efforts to gain additional tax support.

Ten years ago, many public colleges and universities were involved in development; there is little evidence that it has affected their ability to justify adequate tax support. What is required is a careful definition of what private funds will be used for, and public libraries should have little difficulty in segregating public funds for basic support from private funds which can be used to strive for excellence. The search for funds from corporations, foundations, and private donors is also important in gaining access to the community's decision makers, and it is essential for communication of the library's goals and objectives.

Several years ago, when I was director of the Columbus Public Library in Ohio, we were faced with a serious financial problem which threatened to close a third of the system's branch libraries. To ensure that an objective analysis was undertaken to determine which branches to close, a major local foundation was approached to obtain a modest grant to retain an outside consultant. It was the first time the library ever approached the foundation, and its board and officials were curious to learn about the library and its problems. Funds were subsequently approved for the study, and a formula was proposed to determine which branches to close.

However, some essential contacts were made with community leaders as a result of the foundation's small grant, and these leaders suggested that a public referendum might be tried as an alternative to closing the branches. With that encouragement and participation, endorsements were gained from the media, citizen organizations, and other community leaders which subsequently resulted in a successful election for a tax increase of more than 50 percent. The branches did not have to be closed. Service could be expanded. A permanent Friends of the Library organization was established by the participants in that election campaign. And, the major foundation was so impressed by the results of its first small grant that it subsequently provided a substantial grant which allowed the library to purchase an automated circulation control system.

Leadership cultivates other leadership in the city, and the effective administrator finds him/herself involved in many activities and organizations which provide contact essential for influencing decisions favorably toward the library.

Contracting for services is another area that is rarely considered by library administrators, and that is unfortunate. Several years ago, I directed a medium-sized public library on the outskirts of Cleveland. Nearby was a regional headquarters for the National Aeronautics and Space Administration and located there was the midwest film library for NASA. I learned that the agency was seeking to contract out the responsibility for managing this film library, and, since the library I administered at that time had some experience in administering a cooperative film circuit, we submitted a proposal. As it turned out, it was the lowest bid, and we were awarded a contract with NASA to circulate its films at a specific rate per circulation. This occurred right at the time of the lunar missions, and every school, college, library, and organization in 11 states was trying to obtain the first films on the lunar missions. Before long, the revenues from this contract were providing more than one-third of our budget.

There is no reason why public libraries cannot draw upon their experience in handling resources and information to creatively supplement their normal tax income. The line between private business and public service is becoming more murky each day, and there is room for more initiative by public administrators in furnishing some services that may be ignored by the private sector.

Before we leave the issue of leadership in financing libraries, some mention should be made about the practice of fighting city hall. When libraries receive word that the city administration intends to reduce their budget, or reject any increase, there is often a tendency for leadership to manifest itself in the form of angry criticism of the administration or in a fight for restoration by Friends and similar organizations.

A library administrator has to be careful to provide the right type of leadership in this situation. S/he owes loyalty to that administration, just as s/he must fully support the policies of the library board. If the library director cannot accept those decisions and seek to implement them, then s/he should not continue in that position. That does not mean that the library administrator should not seek to influence those decisions in the best interests of the organization s/he represents. Nor should the administrator seek to misrepresent the city council or the board to community groups which may wish to help restore some of those cuts. Good communication is essential if the community is to know why the city council or board made those decisions. From there, it is up to the community group to take any initiative, not the library director.

Leadership demands the strength and intelligence to fight like hell for the budget the library needs, but, if that fight is lost, to carry out the result of that decision to the best of the individual's ability. It also demands playing it straight for the board or city council with the community. Then once the community has the facts, it is the community's responsibility to present its position to the board or the city administration.

NEW SERVICES

Mention was previously made about the importance of initiation of new services. Besides the impact upon staff morale and the improved image of the library that is created, there are tangible benefits which are possible through the elimination of less effective services and attraction of new users. But, before any new service is implemented, consideration should be first given to the identification of a need for this service. It rarely comes directly from the community, and, in fact, most user surveys demonstrate that the typical user is satisfied with the present services the library may offer. There is no clear pattern or explanation for the origin of new and innovative library services, just as there are few explanations for a new product which may evolve in the commercial sector. Marketing surveys or studies may provide some idea as to the acceptance of a new service, but they do not generate new services of themselves.

In reviewing my experience over the 20 years I have been in library service, it has been my observation that new services have their origins in individuals who are faced with problems which cannot be solved by traditional means. It may be the lack of usage by a particular group in the community or a frustration over the lack of resources suitable to satisfy some request. I recall the origin of a very successful medical information and referral service. Staff complained about the lack of medical reference materials suitable for the layperson. The solution was a tape library prepared with the aid of the local medical society. Impressed by the success of this effort, the local bar association decided to copy this service for common legal questions.

Leadership is a necessity if new ideas are not to be stifled and if they are to become reality. Some successful new services have been made possible only because the library administrator could meet frequently and informally with the staff in an atmosphere where individuals felt free to broach ideas and others felt free to contribute to them. Brainstorming can be too free-form and not constructive, but, if the administrator has the talent to focus the attention of the group on a specific problem or need, and direct the discussion toward practical solutions, then one would soon emerge.

Encouraging the emergence of new ways to approach problems is only one aspect of leadership. The next step is to gain general acceptance and, after that, to secure the funding necessary to implement the idea. It has been my experience that innovative solutions to problems (in the form of new services) rarely are difficult to finance. The idea is usually attractive enough to sell itself. It is only when seeking support for the same tired service or solution that one runs into difficulty.

LEADERS AND PEOPLE

It is true that leadership is essential in the securing of adequate financing for the institution; nonetheless, it is with the management of personnel that we most frequently associate leadership. It has been theorized that effective leaders are those individuals who make their followers feel more powerful and influential.[4] If that theory is correct, then the secret is to delegate as much power and responsibility as possible to one's staff. In fact, that is a very common concept in motivation. Unfortunately, it does not always work. Some employees simply do not want more responsibility.

There is another theory which is based upon the analysis of the behavior of the effective leader. Researchers concentrate on what effective leaders do, rather than on what they are.[5] Invariably, this research ends in an analysis of managerial style and of the factors which led the individual to fully delegate power and authority in one instance and to dictate a direct action in another instance.

Leadership is the art of determining when to do either, and it is based on the nature of the task and the knowledge of the individual or group who will have to undertake that task. R. R. Blake and J. S. Mouton have attempted in the management literature to convert this into an automatic formula which the typical administrator may use to simplify the process.[6] Helpful though a formula may be, few executives have the luxury of time to analyze all the factors necessary for each of their decisions.

Most administrators are either task- or people-oriented. In the first instance, they realize the importance of the task and can define the steps necessary to achieve it. That does not imply a callous disregard for people as much as a stress on an analytical skill. The people-oriented administrator is sensitive, on the other hand, to the capabilities of his/her personnel and will seek to match the task to the individual and even remodel the task if the individual requires that attention. The result may be an inherent inefficiency but an improved morale. Effective leadership achieves a balance between a concern for the task and people. As noted earlier, one definition of leadership is getting things done, and things get done better and faster if there is a concern for completing the task and satisfying the unique needs of the individual.

In practice, an effective leader has no single management style. S/he has an array of approaches or a repertoire which is employed depending upon the nature of the task and the human resources available. There is yet another management formula developed by P. Hersey and K. H. Blanchard that is built on this and is known as situational leadership.[7] It attempts to divide each problem into task and human relationship components. For example, a problem which has a low task and low human relationship factor would indicate the use of a democratic management style. An instance where the task was very important and human relationships were of little concern would dictate an autocratic style.

Useful though these formulas may be, the administrator of the large public library is rarely confronted with the type of problem which can be categorized that conveniently. S/he is usually left to judge the importance of the problem or task and establish an appropriate priority. Invariably, it has a high priority, or it would never have reached him/her. The administrator then must assess the skills and strengths of the staff, and, once again, there are likely to be few capable to deal with the assignment.

CONCLUSION

In this imperfect environment, the administrator is left only with a range of compromises. Leadership is demonstrated when those compromises are adequate to the task and satisfactory to those assigned.

Leaders must also have a thorough understanding of motivation and realize that those individuals who are most effective in dealing with a problem or task are those who are able to develop their own solutions or methods and who see some growth for themselves in the process of handling that assignment.

Thus far, I have reviewed several definitions of leadership and discussed various factors which affect leadership in the context of the larger public library. Much of this essay has been devoted to strategies which will result in effective leadership. Some discussion occurred about the role of the library administrator in influencing the image of the library and the importance of that image. With regard to funding, leadership was considered in relation to developing strategies for finding alternative sources of income. The process of initiating new services was also reviewed from the perspective of the role that leadership plays in the development and implementation of those services. And, the methods that leadership exercises in personnel relations were considered.

Since the focus of this book is upon the role of leadership through the end of the twentieth century, I want to end with some observations upon leadership strategies in the large public library to the year 2000. Whatever skills and experience were essential during the past several decades will be even more essential during the coming years. If resources have been limited, they will become even more limited in the coming years. If staff are less willing to accept only delegated authority at present, they will come to require authority as an earned right in the future. If facilities are less capable of serving present needs, conditions will only further deteriorate in the future.

Leadership will have to gain keener insight to human needs in our complex cities if it is to remain ahead of the crest of the avalanche. To accomplish that, the library administrator will have to draw more and more upon the specialized resources of other planning organizations in the city and establish even closer linkage with the leadership at the neighborhood level. Communication between the front line public service units of the library system will have to be redesigned to provide more rapid and more accurate feedback. We certainly see this being achieved with the online circulation systems which will be capable of furnishing the management information essential for the definition of trends in the use and demand for specific resources. Similar feedback will need to be developed in information services provided to the community and in cultural and educational programming.

In an era of decreasing resources, certainly greater leadership will be required in the formation of coalitions to make optimum use of newer technology. We have witnessed considerable cooperation in fields such as cable television, but that is only the beginning, and, if libraries are not to be forgotten and left out of the mainstream of the positive changes which will be taking place in our cities, library administrators will have to hustle and demonstrate much more involvement in the civic life of the great cities.

In the title of this essay, I referred to the library leader as a warrior and philosopher. The fight for funds, recognition, participation, and flexibility is certain to become more difficult and demand greater strength in the future. As the library is forced to evolve in response to changing public usage and limited resources, it is essential that the executive have a solid philosophy of emerging library service and the power to communicate that new role to governance, staff, and the public.

The American public library is one of our unique contributions to history, and our large urban public library systems are the pinnacle of that achievement. Whatever will be the ultimate fate of any type or size of library will first befall the large public library.

One of the most consistent debates in understanding leadership is whether leaders create change or change creates leaders. Whatever the answer to that debate may be, there can be little doubt that America's larger public libraries are indeed undergoing great change. I am confident of their survival, and I am equally confident that leadership will exist in the future which will not be satisfied with mere survival.

REFERENCES

1. John R. Rizzo, *Management for Libraries: Fundamentals and Issues* (Westport, CT: Greenwood Press, 1980), p. 297.

2. V. H. Vroom and P. W. Yetton, *Leadership and Decision Making* (Pittsburgh: University of Pittsburgh Press, 1973), p. 316.

3. Rizzo, p. 297.

4. Rizzo, p. 300.

5. Rizzo, p. 303.

6. R. R. Blake and J. S. Mouton, *The Management Grid* (Houston, TX: Gulf Publishing Co., 1964), p. 11.

7. P. Hersey and K. H. Blanchard, *Management of Organizational Behavior: Utilizing Human Resources* (Englewood Cliffs, NJ: Prentice Hall, 1977), p. 15.

Doomsday or Camelot?

by Harold G. Lord

If, indeed, the past is prologue, any self-respecting soothsayer surveying the school library/media program would have the crystal ball for the future quickly covered with soot. The factors which led to the rapid developments for school library/media programs during the 60s and the 70s are factors which no longer exist in the schools of the United States. The times are changin', and no place are they changing more than in the process of education in the public schools.

The 60s and 70s brought rapid growth to the school library/media program. We shared in federal funding; we shared in the attention that dollars brought; we shared in federal funding; we shared in the attention that dollars brought; we shared in curriculum experimentation; we reaped the benefits of the baby boom to expand our resources and our services; we served on advisory committees; we developed guidelines; and we published standards. We met with other school library/media professionals (educational media specialists) and convinced ourselves that we were change agents, but we frequently overemphasized service to the detriment of instruction and we spent our budget on items such as 16 mm sound film projectors, overhead projectors, tape recorders, video recorders, etc. We increased our inventory of ''stuff'' and attempted to show others how to use the new equipment effectively. We convinced ourselves that life in Camelot was beautiful, and we would live happily forever and ever. But, throughout all this activity, we, as educational media specialists, did not really convince the decision makers of our invincibility as an element of the school program.

For years, the profession has been telling us that we were change agents. National conventions, regional meetings, symposiums, and position papers on school library/media activities have reflected the emerging role of the educational media specialist. But, that role has been demonstrated in very few instances. Attempts to make changes have frequently been dissipated as school personnel became caught up in the minutia of getting *this* item to *that* place. So engrained were we with the four Rs of library/media technology (i.e., the Right material at the Right place, at the Right time, used in the Right way) that time and effort never allowed us to perform the tasks of change agents.

Betty Fast has described the traditional school library as follows:

> No one ever accused the traditional school library of revolutionary tendencies; its serene and studious atmosphere epitomized a passive role in the educational scene. Its function was to support the curriculum of the school in a subservient handmaiden fashion. The leadership that a few outstanding librarians managed to demonstrate in their schools came despite and not because of their positions.[1]

Although we have frequently deluded ourselves into accepting new and different challenges and other roles (i.e., to preserve and to protect that which is good, to improve that which is mediocre, and to create that which is lacking), our creative efforts have been too infrequently directed toward these dimensions.

As educational media specialists, we have known intuitively that our programs were essential to the learning environment of the school, but few of us have done the kinds of program appraisal that could provide the informational data to preserve an endangered area within the school program. Boards of education and superintendents of schools, caught in budgetary crunches, have frequently opted to eliminate professional positions and replace them with paraprofessionals, stretching their dollars by providing more people power in service areas but diminishing the amount of professional interaction with the students.

Somewhere on the road through Camelot, we failed to turn, to give direction, and to solidify our worth, and we failed to utilize time for basking in the sunlight to our best advantage. Maybe our foray in the future will be better.

With lost changes behind us, let us look at some of the factors that will affect the school library/media programs of the next two decades.

ENROLLMENT

The baby boom is over. Many school districts are experiencing a decrease in enrollment, which has led an increasing number of school districts to face a reduction in force. One program which absorbs its share of these reductions is the school library/media program.

CURRICULUM DEVELOPMENT

The curriculum experimentations/innovations of the past decade have not been validated and have led to criticism. The watchword now is back-to-basics. Emphasis is being placed on eliminating frills. Unfortunately, some citizens feel that the school library/media program is one of those frills. "All those movies; we never had movies and television when I went to school" is a common expression of the advocates for reduced programs.

SCHOOL ENVIRONMENT

The school library/media center should be, in the most explicit sense, at the center of instructional activities. As a physical place, it provides space for the instructional resources which support the curriculum, but the campus of the future is changing with the advent of open schools, universities-without-walls, and the inner-city high rises. Technology has expanded far beyond the confines of four walls. In the techno-age of Toffler's "electronic cottage,"[2] the sources of information are changing so rapidly that the physical environment of a school library/media center must also change in the future so that it is able to encompass the outreaching of the electronic age. The access points for delivery systems may still remain physical places, such as the school library/media centers, through microcomputer modems and cablevision receivers; however, information will be readily available throughout our environment.

SPECIAL CHILD

The role of the educational media specialist in these future years will still be in the areas of instruction, curriculum development, and acquisition of resources. The reemphasis on the basics will most likely be an impetus overshadowing the efforts made in the 70s toward special educational programs for handicapped or gifted youngsters. Our apparent neglect of the average student will be rectified. The child, as an unique individual, will be greatly reemphasized.

FUNDING

The reductions in federal funding will have a significant impact on library services. Many of the school library/media programs have been developed solely on ESEA and NDEA funds, and few programs will have this money replaced by local funds. Most services for school library/media programs offered by state departments of education have been supported by federal funding; in fact, most states have done little or nothing by way of state funding to provide local districts with appropriate state leadership, even though state funding for education represents a goodly portion of revenue at the local school district level.

NETWORKING

School personnel are anxious to cooperate in networking but are bound by some restrictive policies propagated by local boards of education and by federal purchasing regulations. The sharing of resources, especially the vast collections of audiovisual materials, is a situation that each locale must resolve. We discover that schools can become full-scale participants in interlibrary cooperation when they focus on the strengths to be gained by joining multitype library systems rather than on the problems that their memberships might create. As Falsone has stated: "Certainly much more is gained by direct attention to the strengths that school libraries can contribute rather than spending time lamenting the limitations that often inhibit library cooperation with schools."[3] The role for schools in networking has been the topic of various publications.[4]

LEARNING PATTERNS

The school library/media program is vital to education because of our increased knowledge of the way youngsters learn. If schools are to move from a classroom- and teacher-dominated routine (which has already been declared outmoded by the students) to a learner-oriented environment, the media center must emerge as a key component of the learning process. Media must play an active, not a passive, role in the school experience. The success of students will depend largely on the way learners use resources. They must be able to find, to evaluate, and to apply information.

Without a doubt, the teaching of media skills will become the most important role of the educational media specialist in the next decade. This instruction will not be just limited to how to manipulate information but will include how to creatively express the student's viewpoint through the use of media.

ADAPTATION OF TECHNOLOGY

Much has been written about the future impact of communications technology. For example, *Next Magazine,* a periodical devoted to a look into the future, devoted its February 1981 issue to the media decade.[5] All of the forecasters suggest multichannel bombardment as part of the information explosion. As new technology comes forward, we will be able to harness this explosive force more readily in order to disseminate it to the users.

Through all of this change, the educational system has always seemed to be last to accept new ideas, to adopt the research, or to implement the technology. School officials in the past have frequently been led by Pied Pipers of the latest fad, seeking a panacea for all the ills of our educational process. Some of these fads were the weapons to fight off the barbs and criticisms of a supposedly failing educational system. In turn, the technology of television, teaching machines, the new math curriculum, and calculators, along with the computer, have had their turns. The most promising of the newer developments, especially in the area of instructional technology, has been the paragon of instructional design which combines the best of what we have learned from programmed instruction and the use of technology.

Some people refer to children as the resources of a nation, tomorrow's promise, and the hope of civilization. Others label children as juvenile delinquents, welfare recipients, tax burdens, or wards of the state. Still others think only in terms of noisy-Norris, Sally who sings, or Johnny of blond-curls, an angelic smile, and the soul of a fiend. The obligation to educate, to train, and to inform is still the basic function of the schools. That function will be influenced by the electronic information age. The role of the educational media specialist will be to assist that plugged-in child to learn best how to utilize those vast resources. Where is King Arthur when we need him most?

REFERENCES

1. Betty Fast, "The Media Specialist as an Agent for Change," *Wilson Library Bulletin* 49 (May 1975): 636–37.

2. Alvin Toffler, *The Third Wave* (New York: William Morrow, 1980), p. 10.

3. Anne Marie Falsone, "Participation of School Libraries," *Multitype Library Cooperation*, eds. Beth Hamilton and William Ernst (New York: Bowker, 1977), p. 137.

4. National Commission on Libraries and Information Science, *The Role of the School Library Media Program in Networking* (Washington, DC: NCLIS, 1978).

5. "The Media Decade," *Next Magazine* 2 (February 1981): pp. 27–62.

Leadership in the Community/Junior College Library

by Sheryl Anspaugh

Among the unanswered questions about leadership are: How much, if at all, does the environment control a leader? Will a successful leader in one situation be equally effective in another? Does each new environment offer the same probability for successful leadership or does the environmental mix of organizational tradition, the organization's people, the legal authority, the clients, and the location of the institution strongly influence the result of leadership?

It is with these questions in mind, and the belief that environment plays a major role, that I have divided the essay into two parts: first, a discussion of the community/junior college setting with an emphasis on its unique qualities; and second, an exploration of library leadership in this setting and in general.

ENVIRONMENT

Community/junior colleges developed from educational needs that were not being met by traditional four-year schools. The traditional two-year college or prep school, which was academically oriented and served as an intermediate step to the university, was the first to be established. During the last 15-20 years, communities have given authorization and funding for community colleges to provide comprehensive adult learning centers in an effort to meet local educational needs. Thus, the community college movement has been closely aligned to the changing economical and educational needs of the community and of the student. The financial and political backing of the business community has assisted in obtaining needed legislation and funding and has provided a guaranteed market for many of the graduates.

An increase in leisure time activities and the vast sums of money spent for leisure activities have not been overlooked by the community college, as can be seen by the dozens of recreational, self-improvement noncredit courses. In addition, strictly technical or trade schools have evolved and expanded into the more encompassing role of the community college, taking advantage of the new importance of being skilled or certified in the technologically sophisticated 70s and 80s. Presently, most community/ junior colleges combine the trade, vocational, technical, and occupational two-year degree or certificate program with an academic program. This shift of emphasis was a direct result of businesses and industries needing skilled, trained personnel and the accompanying wage increases.

The students—especially the minority student who has had difficulty in being admitted to a university, the housewife who is going back to work, the white-collar worker who wants to work on his/her car, and the laborer who wants to upgrade his/her job—have all found a place in the community college. A symbiotic relationship—based on economics and benefits to all involved groups: the students, the community, and the college—has profoundly influenced the rapid growth of the community college business in less than two decades. It is this mutual set of needs that has allowed the community college to set up a tax base and governing board. Through a property or sales tax, state and federal funds, and student tuition, substantial community colleges with all the accoutrements of a small university campus have been developed. Two exceptions, and perhaps they suggest an alternative to financing, are Austin (Texas) Community College and Houston (Texas) Community College System. In both cases, neither a tax base nor an independent governing authority was established. These two colleges are funded as extensions to the high schools; they share facilities, being high schools during the day and college campuses at night. Funding is based on state and federal appropriations, student tuition, and a budget set aside from local taxes raised to support the school system. Additionally, the two colleges share their governing boards with the school systems (for example, the same board members serve Houston Independent School District *and* Houston Community College System). The same board members meet at different times and locations, depending on whether they are meeting for the school board or the college board. This arrangement can work, evidenced by ten years of existence for the Houston Community College System and eight years for the Austin Community College.

Regardless of how the school is funded, or who is on its board, the mission of community/junior colleges is substantially the same, and it reflects the general mission of education at large. The mission of the community/junior college differs only in that it serves everyone from the little tyke who is the subject of a day care training program to the elderly or institutionally confined. The non-English-speaking student, the adult basic education learner, the university bound student, and the prison inmate are all examples of community college students. Classes in computer training and secretarial skills are offered at a student's place of work; nursing home residents can enjoy a full range of classes as the community college goes to the student.

The revised mission statement, predicated on economics and declining student population, is becoming: "If you want it, we've got it or we'll get it—tell us where and when." Another trend, based on economics, that is developing is the use of shared resources and shared facilities. These ideas are not new; the itinerant teacher/philosopher and the students gathering around the teacher wherever s/he might be goes back to the earliest teaching/learning settings. It was only later that formal universities of bricks and mortar became a reality.

Today, we may have to reevaluate our thinking and look back to some old ways with new twists for presenting education. The cost of new bricks and mortar is becoming prohibitive; traveling to "school" in large metropolitan areas is becoming expensive due to high gasoline prices and impossible due to snarled traffic. To for-profit companies, time is money; for them, bringing the teacher to the place of work rather than sending individual workers to a teacher is more economical. Decisions on new ways of dispensing education are being devised, and libraries need to be ready to innovate and adapt library services and resources to the meet the challenges of the 80s.

Certainly, one of the challenges will be the flux and uncertainty of the community/junior college direction. Community/junior colleges are trying to serve everyone, to meet all needs. There is no tradition and very little precedence for them to use as guidelines. Community/junior colleges have experimented with open admissions, flexible entry, classes held in the classroom and in the factory, and one building vs multiple campuses. The diversity of programs and purposes is in a state of flux. Meeting immediate needs may make it difficult to pin down lines of authority and responsibility. One believes that the ability to lead must be influenced by the dynamic and shifting trends in the still-developing community colleges.

A very basic model of organizational change that would apply to community/junior college libraries was developed by Kurt Lewin. He saw change in organizations as having a three-cycle stage of development: (1) thawing, (2) changing, and (3) refreezing.[1] Each stage is important for healthy change and growth, giving an organization time to evaluate (thawing), to implement (changing), and to incorporate change (refreezing).

Keeping the library organization balanced in its change can be the difference between frustration and challenge. It will be incumbent upon leaders to balance responsiveness to needs with planned change.

Who is the community college student? It is anyone, except those who are 5-18 years of age; that age range does not delineate it by much (a mere

13 years out of 75-80 years). The diversity of the community college clientele requires a library that is closer to a public library in attitude, service, and resources than it is to a four-year college library. The spread of ages, interests, reading skills, and college curricula demands of a plethora of materials—childrens books; Vietnamese-English dictionaries; human skeletons; Resusi Annies; and books and media on technical report writing, printing, plumbing, roofing, drafting, and auto mechanics. The community college library takes on qualities of the special library with staff requiring knowledge of technical standards and unique research tools. And, it is a college library, like any other, that must provide resources for papers/reports assigned in English, science, history, philosophy, the arts, and psychology courses.

The community college library needs the support of its three groups of clients: administrators, faculty, and students. Despite public relations brochures and student handbooks, which refer to them as the ''center of education,'' libraries have had an uphill battle to serve clients (many of whom are reluctant users) and to get their support. Of course, this is not unique to community/junior college libraries. Repeated user studies show public and academic library use to be limited, resulting in a prevalent problem of use and support that concerns library leaders.

Administrative support of the budget is mandatory, faculty respect for the library's role in the educational process is vital, and student use is the reason for existence. Library leaders must understand and articulate the relationship between the library and the classroom to ensure support and funding of the library. The fact that the relationship between the two areas rarely exists has created a vicious cycle within the educational process. No doubt for some schools, libraries exist only to promote sanctioning by an accrediting agency. This lack of understanding of the library's role, coupled with limited funds, leaves room for noncommitment. As a result, the library program becomes vulnerable, more so than in institutions, such as four-year colleges, with the traditional humanities programs. The library clients need to be educated about libraries or the probability of reduced funding will increase.

The emphasis for changes in the 80s in community/junior colleges will focus on shared facilities/resources, technology, and teaching methods.

SHARED FACILITIES AND COOPERATIVE AGREEMENTS

The concept of shared facilities and cooperative agreements are beginning to develop and will gain momentum as taxpayers want more utilization of existing resources. An indication of this trend was the mandate from the White House Conference on Libraries and Information Science. But, it involves far more than sharing a high school library or borrowing books from another library. The problem is with people who have a need for territorial rights and a repugnance of joint ownership and dual responsibility. The problem will be with mergers: who is boss, what's yours, what's mine, what's ours. Also, the problem will be with clients who need and want the information now and not in the next delivery. These will be the difficult issues for library leaders to overcome and administer.

"Matrix" is the term for this type of organizational arrangement.[2] It is contrary to the more familiar arrangement known as hierarchy. But, beyond the identifying terms, there is little of concrete value on how to manage a matrix organization. This new concept has worked well in limited situations, but it has yet to be proven as a workable long-term organizational concept. To the taxpayer, a building in use during the day as a high school and at night as a college, using the same desks, chalkboards, and library books, must make sense. This dual operation can coexist if guidelines and communication are established. Houston Community College System and Houston Independent School District have 10 shared facilities. A commitment to the concept of joint library use has overcome the complications of using both Dewey Decimal and Library of Congress classification systems, limited space for additional shelving and materials, a difference in operating style, different qualifications for staffing, security, equipment maintenance, length of borrowing privileges, and who charges overdue fines for which books to which students at how much a day. The library directors have worked with principals, area superintendents, and librarians. Flexibility, sensitivity, innovation, and above all, patience have been the leadership qualities required in this situation.

The potential monsters of shared use have been one by one tamed through the adoption of guidelines, the ability to listen, and lots of effort and time in tackling each problem. The shared use concept can work, and more libraries are investigating shared use plans. Shared use is not limited to high schools and community colleges. Public libraries and university libraries are tax-supported institutions, so why not expand their use on a shared basis? Through a cooperative effort between Houston Community College System, Houston Independent School District, and Houston Public Library, the holdings of the public library (on microfiche catalogs) have been placed in high school libraries and 21 community college libraries. Faculty and students now have a million additional volumes at their fingertips, as they can call to have a book sent through a delivery service in operation by Houston Community College System or ask the branch library to hold the material for them.

Another area in which Houston Community College System has advantage of existing resources for its diverse faculty and student population is through the establishment of cooperative agreements with the University of Houston and the Rice University libraries. In the cooperative agreement with Rice, a librarian from Rice is paid by Houston Community College System to provide weekend professional reference service to all who use the library.

Books, media, equipment, shelving, staff, lighting, and air conditioning are increasingly more expensive, thus, forcing upon us a reevaluation of the traditional maxim of library service, ''the right book to the right person at the right time.'' This maxim can remain true, but only through considerable planning for flexibility on everyone's part. It takes several dynamic, forward-thinking individuals pulling in the same direction to bring forth a functional sharing system.

EDUCATIONAL TECHNOLOGY

Educational technology (nonprint media, hardware, and appropriate applications) has been around for years and is now a strong component of most community/junior college libraries. It includes video and audio cassettes, transparencies, computer-assisted instruction, filmstrips, filmloops, and all the action, color, and visuals that result from a television age. Educational technology is no longer a ''passing fad'' in higher education, despite the resistance of university libraries to incorporate it. Houston Community College System library has opened its film collection for use by university professors, as well as by Houston area business and industry. Requests have been so numerous that a booking system that reserves films as much as a year in advance requires the attention of a full-time staff member. Community/junior college libraries have seen the value of the multimedia approach and offer it to faculty and students as teaching/learning aids. Audiovisual media have become another library format that community/junior college librarians can recommend and make referrals to, just as they do print materials.

Community colleges from California to Florida are offering classes in the student's home via cable TV; some of these schools are producing quality material for their own use and for sale. With the newest ''toy'' video equipment, classroom instruction can be filmed and then replayed as many times as needed for the student to grasp and master that segment of learning. Audio cassettes allow typing, shorthand, and languages to be practiced at home, on a lunch hour, or at other places/times. All of this and more is possible, and library leaders can become central to yet another aspect of the learning process. Students can check out books and/or media from the library. Or, if they want their own copies, duplication of audio and video cassettes is free to all students and faculty of the 21 Houston Community College System campuses (provided copyright release has been obtained). A request for media use or duplication is as easy and quick as requesting a book. The videodisc may replace video cassette, but, more importantly, media technology will permit more emphasis on the individual student, his/her needs, learning patterns, and place and time constraints. The prospects are only limited by the imagination and the budget.

The area of educational technology that includes bibliographical databases probably should remain in the bailiwick of the four-year colleges and universities. Several of these databases (e.g., ERIC, MEDLARS) are seldom used by community/junior college students and faculty. Occasionally, an instructor working on a dissertation requests a computer-assisted search, but most students and faculty are unaware of the most basic sources of information and how to use them. Library users want information that is short and complete and circulating—they want it *now*. Electronic bibliographic searches do not meet that expectation.

The educational nonprint format won't replace books, but it can be found in abundance and quality. It can be prepackaged; it is attention-getting; it can add depth, dimension, and a certain ease to teaching. It can be a boon to the part-time instructor or to the technically skilled class which is appropriate for modular learning.

THE USERS

Today, more people are working, more are working at two jobs, and more are interested in skilled occupations; this social economic phenomenon has an impact on the community college. As the community college population shifts to proportionately more part-time students who require part-time teachers, fewer full-time instructors are needed. This has forced colleges to scramble to come up with qualified part-time instructors and librarians who can rush from full-time work at 4:30 or 5:00 p.m. to teach a part-time class at 6:00 p.m. or to have a branch library open at 5:00 p.m. There is limited planning time and few opportunities for casual meetings; librarians work hard to get even a few minutes with the instructor. Consequently, a high teacher and librarian turnover results. This fragmentation of personnel and communication creates problems in developing and implementing any program either within a department or across departments.

The program of library use instruction, and its components of library awareness and library orientation, have become a hot library topic, but they may be especially difficult to implement in a fragmented or dispersed community college setting. Library use instruction is in a "Catch 22" spin. College courses of education or any other graduate field do not emphasize or even discuss the integration of library use into the curricula. Even basic tenets of education may be foreign in community colleges, which emphasize the technical trades and rely extensively on part-time instructors. Common sense would indicate that instructors who don't know libraries can't be expected to use them. Libraries need to become an integral part of the curricula and teaching skills, but that is a long-term proposition that will require a major shift of emphasis in our educational process.

Library use instruction, orientation, and awareness is directed first to the instructor and second to the student at Houston Community College System. It was reasoned that, if the faculty became comfortable in using the library and found the staff helpful, then they would bring the students and library together. A second factor in approaching the faculty first was logistical. With a student enrollment of over 32,000 on 21 campuses, sheer numbers forced a decision to concentrate effort on the nearly 1,000 faculty members. This decision prompted a series of efforts to educate the faculty, to make them library users and supporters. A brochure of library services for faculty was designed and distributed (the brochure won an ALA Public Relations honorable mention); each professional librarian has been assigned a teaching division (for example, industrial education, humanities), and that librarian is responsible for collection development, working with individual faculty, attending staff meetings, and doing new instructor orientation. A five-year collection development plan ensures that books/media pertaining to each department within the division are carefully reviewed, weeded, balanced, and rejuvenated every five years.

But, in addition, the library staff has had to become acutely aware of the reading level, or nonreading level, of so many students. Community colleges, who practice an open admissions policy, must employ faculty, counselors, librarians, and staff who are sensitive to the students who cannot speak English well or who have very limited reading and comprehension skills. Retention of these special students must be considered by librarians in their collection development plans.

LEADERSHIP

Leadership is described by James MacGregor Burns as "that most observed and least understood phenomenon."[3]

Leadership in the community/junior college library is generally not different from leadership in any other institution or organization. In my definition, leadership is dependent on: (1) the situation; (2) the tasks at hand; (3) the followers; and (4) the personality and skills of the leader.

These four factors give individuality to each organization, community/junior college libraries not withstanding. However, it is the fourth item that is of special interest, because it is the one that the individual leader has the most control over.

The qualities that most of us attribute to leadership (honesty, intellect, integrity, credibility, empathy, loyalty, respect for others, physical stamina) still hold true for most people, and, recently, the traits of charisma, proper dress, and healthy good looks have been added to the list. On top of all that, library leaders must be able to please a search committee which has as many definitions of leadership as committee members. Leadership is as tenuous and fickle as beauty, being only in the eyes of the holder.

What some people or search committees have come to expect of library leaders is totally out of perspective. All too often, extremes are used in an attempt to identify potential leaders; only a certain set of academic degrees and experience in a particular type of library are established as harsh parameters. Our profession unnecessarily limits its base of potential leaders due to these self-imposed restrictions. One would generally consider a breadth of experience desirable, especially in community/junior college libraries because of their unique clientele. At the other end of the spectrum is the extreme of hiring a generalist nonlibrarian. There are too many examples of the history professor appointed library director and of staffs frustrated by the need to explain the basic tenets and concepts of librarianship in order to continue library service. More often, the mistake (and it is just as serious) is the appointment of a PhD in media or education who does not have the work experience or understanding necessary for managing the complexities of libraries.

A history department or law firm would not hire someone without the basic professional degree. Why do media specialists without library experience become library directors? Is library education too narrow for community colleges? Is the profession lacking in its own self-confidence? What is the perception of administrators and teaching faculty of library staff?

Leadership benchmarks in the community/junior college library profession should include an appropriate education, diverse experience, a curious mind, an appetite for success, an ability to write and speak on and about the profession, and active participation in the profession. With the demands of an economic tightening of the budget and a leveling off or decreasing student enrollment, flexible, innovative community/junior college library leaders are needed more than ever. It is vital that these individuals understand and deal with the connection between causes (college policies, budget restraints, community needs) and effects (shared facilities, media technology). The importance of the library director will be in combining an understanding of the historical background with a comprehension of the dynamics of problem solving.

There are two characteristics of leaders: (1) tenacity of purpose, and (2) quality of decision.

And, there are two types of decisions: (1) problem solving, and (2) planning. Tenacity of purpose equals achieving results. It amounts to careful planning and understanding the position of the college in the community and of the library's relation to the college as perceived by its various clientele (administrators, faculty, students, noncollege groups). It is realizing what will and won't work within the institution. Tenacity of purpose is a game plan, a sense of timing, and study of the human and organizational behavior that constitute the library's environment. The leader is responsible for developing his/her acumen in these areas, but it is important to remember that a network of individuals is an essential and vital source of information for responsible and rational decision making.

Quality decisions in problem solving and planning depend on quality assumptions, which depend on quality information.[4] This information depends on an informational network which should be broadly based among the library's clientele. In a system of change, sensors are needed by the leader to enable him/her to fit together the pieces of the diversified community college puzzle. Changes that affect the library are coming from many directions: e.g., the addition of programs, the opening of a new campus, the termination of a particular course, and/or the implementation of a federally funded program for the unskilled or the refugee. The library needs as much lead time as possible to be prepared in meeting these and other needs. So often, the information comes first, and with the greatest accuracy, through the network, not through the lines of authority.

Therefore, it is incumbent upon the leader and his/her staff to cultivate the resources, to develop library supporters among them, to coopt them into a loyal interest or ''lobby'' group providing information and protecting and insulating the library from ''danger'' (e.g., budget cuts, reduction in staff and hours, loss of space). Thus, decisions will be based on as much information as can practically be absorbed within a limited amount of time. And, since decision-making ability is probably the single most important aspect of a good leader, the quality of the information network can make the difference between a caretaker and a leader.

Graphically, this concept is portrayed as a systems approach to decision making as developed by Easton:[5]

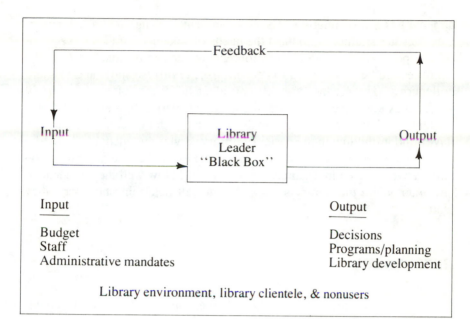

In its concept, the ''black box'' represents the decision maker, who receives input from the environment, rationally applies all this information to the situation, and produces decisions or inputs. The results and/or feedback from these decisions, of course, affect the environment and, in turn, affect the new input. Library leaders must also study the library's impact on users and nonusers. A knowledge of who they serve and how, and of who they do not yet serve and why, is necessary information for understanding the library's environment and for balancing the feedback from the informational network.

True leaders emerge from and return to the wants and needs of their followers. Their task is the recognition and mobilization of their followers' needs. Similar to Maslow's hierarchy of needs, leaders must provide the stimulation, arouse the hopes, aspirations, expectations, and demands of followers. As lower level needs within the organization are met and road-blocks cleared, new needs in expansion of services, resources, development of new curricula, and new roadblocks occur. The job of the leader is to convert problems into opportunities, to inspire people to meet difficult challenges, and to brood creatively about purpose.[6]

Community/junior college library leaders should find the 80s and 90s challenging in their potential, frustrating in their uncertainty, and promising in their outcome. In summary, we have looked at the community/junior college environment and at leadership within this environment, and there appears to be a correlation. The environment is dynamic and changing. Libraries are attempting to meet the needs of students from every segment of the population (readers and nonreaders, academic and vocational). Libraries are being required to decentralize, to diffuse staff, and to share collections. The leaders are self-confident and innovative. They know books; they know media. They understand the relationships among faculty, students, and library. They arouse the demands of followers. These leaders have solid grounding in the basics of library service and media technology; they are attuned to the community and the pressures of the administration and are well-versed in organizational behavior. How well they understand and manipulate the library's environment will determine how well they lead.

REFERENCES

1. Michael Beer, *Organization Change and Development: A Systems View* (Santa Monica, CA: Goodyear Publishing Co., 1980), p. 64.

2. Beer, p. 161.

3. James MacGregor Burns, *Leadership* (New York: Harper and Row, 1978), p. 2.

4. Sidney P. Johnson, "Leading the Way to Success," *Supervisory Management* 24 (September 1979): 10.

5. W. I. Jenkins, *Policy Analysis: A Political and Organizational Perspective* (New York: St. Martin's Press, 1978), p. 61.

6. D. K. Goodwin and J. M. Burns, eds., "True Leadeship," *Psychology Today* 12 (October 1978): 48.

The Courage to Fail

by Edward E. Shaw

Almost 20 years ago, John Gardner wrote that "one of the reasons why mature people are apt to learn less than young people is that they are willing to risk less. Learning is a risky business, and they do not like to fail."[1] Mr. Gardner might well have been writing about organizations of people—universities and libraries, for example—when he said that "by middle age most of us carry in our heads a tremendous catalogue of things we have no intention of trying again because we tried them once and failed, or tried them once and did less well than our self-esteem demanded."[2]

This essay concerns leadership. It concerns leadership in an environment beset with ever lessening resources to undertake an ever increasing set of responsibilities in a era of substantial technological change. In such circumstances, Gardner's warning is poignant: "We pay a heavy price for our fear of failure. It is a powerful obstacle to growth. It assures the progressive narrowing of the personality and prevents exploration and experimentation. There is no learning without some difficulty and fumbling. If you want to keep on learning, you must keep risking failure—all of your life."[3]

There are many definitions of leading, of leadership; the dictionary provides one: "to lead—to guide on a way, especially by going in advance." There are risks "by going in advance." Leaders must accept those risks; they must have the courage to fail.

Our focal point is the library in the research university. A research university is an institution that places relatively greater emphasis, albeit not exclusive, on scholarship, basic research, and graduate education than it does on its other missions (e.g., undergraduate education). Library refers to both the organization and the function. As an organization, the library is a collection of materials, buildings, and people assembled together on a university campus. As a function, the library represents those human, physical, and financial resources the university provides in support of scholarship, basic research, and graduate education. Only occasionally do the organization and the function completely overlap in today's research university.

We will also look briefly at a consortium of research universities, their libraries, and major independent research libraries that have created a partnership called The Research Libraries Group, Inc. (RLG). The motivations, goals, and objectives of RLG have been well-documented elsewhere[4] and will not be repeated here. It suffices to record that these 37 institutions have concluded that they cannot alone provide an adequate flow of scholarly information to support their instruction, research, and public service programs. Whether or not a partnership of relatively homogeneous organizations, by working together, maintain that flow may be demonstrated in the success or failure of RLG.

Among other barriers, the ability to predict the future of research libraries necessitates predicting the future of research universities, an essay, if not a book, in itself. This is so because research libraries do not stand alone, cannot be "planned for" alone, and cannot relate to external forces alone. They are an integral part of a larger entity—the research university—and their future is bound to the future of the university. What we can explore are the forces that impinge upon the research library with greater force and consequence than they do upon the university. How each institution addresses those forces, and how RLG addresses them as well, sets the processes in motion for describing the 90s.

We will, therefore, begin with a brief exploration of the university and its library and follow by setting the stage for the library. We will look at the concept of place, perhaps the greatest challenge to libraries and librarians. Finally, we will explore leadership in the university and in the library during a time of rapid change, showing how, if at all, it relates to a collective activity.

THE UNIVERSITY AND ITS LIBRARY

Most writers about academic organization agree that the university has three primary missions: instruction, research, and public service.

John Millet writes that ". . . universities share in common the purpose of providing instruction to students. Such instruction generally embraces two primary goals: individual self-development and individual student preparation for useful employment in the nation's economy."[5] Recognizing that research is the process for advancing knowledge, he notes that "research fills a dual role . . . it demonstrates, or illuminates that knowledge is dynamic rather than static . . . secondly . . . it provides a knowledge base for the [expansion] of technology . . . [and] for advancing man's understanding of social behavior and social process [and of man himself].''[6] Finally, Millet notes that research and instruction ''are illuminated by public service, by faculty contact with individuals and organizations of society providing the economic, political, professional, and other goods and services essential to individual welfare.''[7]

We use the generic term administration to collect those activities that create the university's infrastructure and allow it to fulfill its three missions. Traditionally, universities via the administrative process have collected and allocated three resources needed to accomplish the missions: human resources, physical resources, and financial resources. Human resources include faculty, students, and staff; physical resources include buildings, laboratories, and the physical library; financial resources include tuition income, grant income, appropriations from legislatures, etc. We use financial resources to assemble human resources and to provide physical resources.

There is a growing recognition that a fourth resource exists: information. It joins the other three as a necessary condition. It includes both scholarly information and administration information, a distinction that is becoming blurred by the advance of technology. As we do with physical resources, we use financial resources to acquire information resources.

Thus, the general context for understanding today's university looks like this:

Mission	Resources
Instruction	Human
Research	Physical
Public Service	Information
	Financial

The matrix formed by the intersection of missions and resources provides a perspective of the university most useful for, among other things, strategic planning.

The library function, as opposed to the library organization, is responsible for the subset of the information resources involving scholarly information. The term library function is used purposefully to reflect the fact that organizations other than the library itself are involved with scholarly information. For example, the computation center assists in the creation, collection and organization, storage and retrieval, and the provision and dissemination of information—roles characteristic of the library.

The library within the research university has four principal functions. It is (1) a symbol, (2) a museum, (3) a center for scholarly information, and (4) a center for information about scholarly information.

The library as a symbol is exemplified by the statement that it is "the heart of the university." Long after the classrooms empty, the dormitories are vacated, the faculty offices and the seminar rooms are left, the library remains as the physical embodiment of the university itself. There are great libraries without great universities, but there are no great universities without great libraries. We treasure the library as the symbol of the university, and correctly so.

As a museum, the library stores and exhibits artifacts of itself and society. Rare books and manuscripts are placed so they can be seen. And, we often use the library as a place to put those papers with which we know not what to do. The library is our archive and our heritage.

As a center for scholarly information, the library plays one of its two traditional and practical roles. It collects, organizes, stores, and provides those materials needed by faculty and students to pursue their work. It serves the people of today and the people of tomorrow.

Finally, the library is a focus for information about information, what today in information science is called meta-information. The card catalog, the reference material, and the bibliographies either provide the library patron with information on where information can be located or provide the patron with facts (e.g., the population of St. Louis in 1920).

We have set the library in the context of the research university. We see that it is a subset of the general university resource called information, and that, as an organization, it has partial responsibility for the component called scholarly information. And, we have shown that the library has four principal functions: two passive—as a symbol and as a museum, and two active—as a center for scholarly information and as a center for information about information. We turn now to the environment within which the university and its library operate.

THE STAGE IS SET

Within the budgets of most universities, there are two line items where the rate of increase of costs exceeds the rate of increase of income to the university: energy and libraries. Within the context presented above, energy is a subset of physical resources. Implicitly or explicitly, the allocation of financial resources for energy, at the rate required, depletes the university's capacity to maintain an adequate flow of resources to the other physical resources components (e.g., building and laboratory renovation).

Similarly, the library is a subset of information resources, and it requires an allocation of financial resources larger than some of the other components. Because libraries dominate the information resources category, if a university is to maintain an adequate flow of scholarly information, it must allocate financial resources to information at the time expense of at least one of the other categories. Typically, resources are reallocated from the physical component first and then from the human resources component, reflected in a lower growth rate of salaries for faculty or staff. Or, and this is the preferred path, the university finds way of increasing the rate of growth of the financial component to produce more financial resources through higher tuition or increased appropriations.

What we are discovering in the 80s is a growing inability to reallocate financial resources (which are unable to maintain a growth rate equal to the rate of inflation) from human or physical resources to information resources. The university must find a way to establish financial equilibrium within its information resources component—a situation whereby the rate of growth of its resource allocation to information is equal to the rate of growth of its overall income. Over the next decade, this could mean allocating, say, 7–10 percent per year (annual growth rate) rather than 12–15 percent per year or even more.

The irony is that the library cannot meet its classical responsibilities with a 15 percent per year growth rate. This is true for three reasons. First, the number of items the library should collect to serve the faculty and student needs is increasing each year. Second, the unit cost of the items is growing faster than inflation—a prime reason being the cost of foreign materials. Third, as the unit costs of materials increase at a rate greater than inflation, faculty and students can purchase fewer items on their own, thus, increasing the demand upon research libraries.

AND THEN, THERE IS INFORMATION TECHNOLOGY

The dominant trend in computer and communications technologies is to place greater and greater capability in the hands of the end users, be they departments or individuals. This trend is clearly seen in the proliferation of minicomputers across the academic campus and in the increased number of personal-professional computers in the hands of faculty and students.

During the last decade, the library used computer technology to mitigate its cost rises. The library's use of data processing has mirrored that of the university and society in general: modest productivity increases in technical processing activities. Some libraries have moved cautiously to use computer technology to support circulation functions, and there are modest beginnings in the creation of online catalogs.

But, like the university itself, the library is faced with a new set of demands from its faculty and its students. With personal computers or department-based minicomputers, university people are demanding entrance into an electronic information network. There is hardly a university not presently attempting to understand and address the concept of "networking the campus."[8] On some campuses, we see text creation support systems—either stand-alone word processors or network-based text services—provided to assist faculty and students. Suddenly, and with increasing momentum, university people are requesting access to only the library's online catalog from their offices, dormitories, or homes. Access to only the local online catalog becomes insufficient when people realize that the present state of communications technology allows them to access the online catalogs of other institutions. The professor of history at Yale is as interested in the catalog of Princeton, Michigan, or New York Public Library as s/he is in his/her own. Our faculty and students have plugs and they expect the university and the library to provide sockets.

The library is unprepared to meet this new demand. It has been so involved with "staying afloat" that it has not had time to undertake any strategic planning. The advent of the personal computer and the computer-based text handling systems (preludes to electronic publishing) is a surprise. And, like the university itself, the library is without the necessary financial capital to adjust to this new electronic world.

THE MEANING OF PLACE

Perhaps the greatest challenge and opportunity for the library within the research university is the beginning phases of a redefinition of place, of geography. For the purposes of this essay, we will assume that the "place" of the university as a geographical entity is secure (i.e., we will not, perforce of the technology, be "distributing the university" before the turn of the century).

One of the more significant characteristics of technological advance in the last 500 years is its effect on time and distance. The advent of movable type altered, fundamentally, our concepts of distance as the barriers to understanding other places dissolved. One historian has noted that the difference between the early and mid-Victorian British empire was the development of the steam engine. The distance between London and India was reduced to the point where central control over foreign policy was feasible. By reducing the time to travel, it became possible for a sense of the empire to evolve into a coherent whole.[9] One could say that the steam engine allowed Queen Victoria to become Empress of India because it reduced the time between London and Bombay. The application of consistent and sustained policy directives became possible. Concepts of time in England changed with the steam locomotive. Most towns essentially went by their own clocks, yet the advent of the train schedule required time to be the same all over England. The sociological effects were fundamental.

The use of the telephone and the development of the commercial jet airplane have had similar effects on our concepts of time and distance. These two developments, along with the steam engine in the 19th century, shared one characteristic in common. They were introduced into society through mechanisms that provided regulations relative to standards, procedures, and safety.

What we are experiencing now—the so-called computer/communications revolution—has been with us only a few years, yet the impact is already substantial and becoming increasingly stronger. At present, the computer with its communications links to anywhere in the world is governed by no standards. On most of our campuses, the great variety of computers cannot "talk" to one another: we have a Computerized Tower of Babel. Strangely, this has been a protection to those professionals concerned with scholarly information, because the "technological" barriers to interconnection have been so great as to reduce to almost zero the demand upon information planners for interconnection. But, "computer populism" may force standards and, if so, then this computer-communications evolution (or revolution) will soon invade the campus with substantial strength.

As we alter our concept of time and distance, we also change our concept of place. One hears more and more about the relocation of the professional workplace to the home. Some companies estimate that as much as 35 percent of their current workforce could work from their homes if an investment in technology, as well as changes in the production functions, were undertaken.[10] Instant communications in written form offered by the computer along with its capacity to store ever increasing amounts of information are already changing our concepts of place. Effective access to information is now possible without leaving one's office, dormitory, or home.

These changes have altered and will continue to alter the concept of the geographical library. The two active functions of the library noted above involved the provision of information and the provision of information about information. Much of this latter function (i.e., meta-information) can be provided via electronic communications. And, if one can locate the information desired, one can use the same technology to have it sent to the office or the home. The library can expect the number of physical transactions it will have with patrons to decrease over the next decade.

The trend suggests the library will become mostly a warehouse from which one plucks, electronically, the material one needs. And, the warehouse need not be close by. If the scholar is at Yale, the warehouse at Michigan is or can be as close as the Beineke Library. The library will become largely passive, acting as a symbol, a museum, and a warehouse. The flow of information, and the capacity to find it in a world where computer populism prevails, requires a strong and effective professional body of talented people.

LEADERSHIP AND STRATEGIC PLANNING

What is needed is leadership, planning, and the courage to fail. Professor Victor Ferkiss has written:

> Freedom consists in responding autonomously and authentically to the currents of life and action passing through one; the loss of freedom is not the loss of an impossible complete self-determination . . . but a synonym for being bypassed and not being allowed to play one's part in shaping the whole.[11]

As is the case for the individual, so it is for the organization or the function. Leadership in this sense is the quest for freedom, the ability to avoid being bypassed, and the courage to go in front. Essential to leadership is planning, because, as Ferkiss continues, "planning is the self-consciousness of the human element in developing patterns of interrelation—a self-consciousness that alone makes control and therefore freedom possible."[12] As we proceed through the next 10 years, the principal, if not sole, responsibility of the research librarian, and particularly the research library director, is to exert leadership, to guide the library and the university through what shall be an extraordinary time.

It was suggested earlier that the library organization is a subset of the library function, which in turn is a subset of the more general university-wide information resource. It is at this level that the research library director and the library's senior staff must lead, at least for the component relating to scholarly information. If the library organization and its officers are not responsible for the library function on a university campus, then who is? And, if the library function is not responsible for scholarly information, then what is? There is no escaping the responsibility; this is a unique opportunity to contribute fundamentally to the intellectual health and survival of the university itself.

To lead in this context is not simple because the issues are complex. As one speaker noted about complexity:

> Of course some people, faced with the fact of complexity, simply reject it, and choose a far more attractive explanation for whatever has gone wrong: conspiracy. This has the advantage of reintroducing the human element, the cause of our problem is not some mysterious failure of social or technical machinery, but malign human intent, a phenomenon we are bound to recognize if only because none of us is immune from it.[13]

More often than is justifiable, we hear that the reason it is so difficult to manage, and much less lead, is that someone doesn't care or doesn't understand or doesn't believe libraries are important. While such a view does tend to simplify the issues, it fails to resolve any problems. More damning, it is passively defensive in character; it is the failure to lead.

For a library in the research university, the issues to be confronted over the next 10 years are complex; they are not subject to easy answers nor will answers, other than brutal ones, be provided by anyone who is not part of the library function. As Millet has written, "the task of leadership . . . is to provide the essential linkage between management and governance. Management must undertake the required planning, involving all managers of the organization . . . the governance structure must make the decisions about purposes, policies, programs, and resources. Management is joined to governance by a structure and process of leadership."[14]

Leadership and management must increasingly be both effective and efficient. Effective means they do the right things; efficient means they do things right. Strategic planning (i.e., multiple-year planning) is one of the more powerful tools of the leader who is also a manager. In the context of this essay, the view must be a long one for the research library director, because it is the only method for internalizing short-term rapid change.

As it relates to information, consider what the research university may be like in 1990. Most, if not all, faculty, students, and staff will have a personal-professional computer or a terminal. In any event, they will have linkage to the university's information network. While not all of the library's bibliographic data will have been converted to machine-readable form, the proportion that will be available is substantial and growing at an increasing rate. The university's network will allow the preparation and storage of text and, by linkage to external networks, will provide the means for faculty to share work-in-progress with colleagues at peer institutions. Information databases, providing answers to most questions of fact and location, will be readily available to scholars. The costs of these services will be borne largely by the university through productivity increases allowed by electronic technology and by a reallocation of resources from service areas no longer needed by the faculty.

The foregoing is a rather conservative perspective of the research university in 1990, at least compared to many futuristic perspectives. What is the place, the role, the function of the library organization in such an environment? No answer is proposed other than the assertion that only through a serious and concerted effort at strategic planning will the library be able to do its part in shaping that future.

How does one begin a strategic planning effort? Each university and each library has its unique ethos that must be acknowledged and imbedded in any substantial attempt at strategic planning. The literature is rich with material on planning; unfortunately, the research library director cannot directly apply the processes used in "the commercial world." There must be a translation in order for administrators and faculty to understand and accept planning.

One must begin with the goals, objectives, or missions of the university itself. Without this general context, any attempt at strategic planning for the library is doomed to fail. This is so because the general context provides the capacity for translation of library strategic planning into university-wide strategic plans. Presented earlier in this essay is a conceptual perspective of the university that places information, and scholarly information, into a general context. For any specific university, there may be a more appropriate general context; the point is that one must be constructed and accepted within the institution.

The most important point is for the "principal librarian" to assume, actively, responsibility for what we have called scholarly information. Strategic planning must be focused upon scholarly information, not on the library organization, as is too often the case. The forces impinging upon today's university place planning for the library organization as simply an operational issue akin to the size of the next increment to the central steam plant. The issue at hand is strategic planning for scholarly information.

The "principal librarian" is in a unique position to assert responsibility for scholarly information. His/her profession is accountable for the organization of information and knowledge. The library is historically and culturally the focal point for our collective attempts within the university at maintaining the flow of scholarly information on the campus. No other university officer can or is likely to exert the leadership needed to address these issues.

Proceeding from information to scholarly information, the next major divisions for planning purposes are (1) creation, (2) collecting and organizing, (3) preserving and storing, and (4) providing and disseminating. The library has seldom addressed creation; but, the evolution of technology leads inevitably to an integration of these four functions. Scholarly information does not recognize any substantive differences among these four activities and neither should strategic planning.

The next major dimension for planning purposes addresses intra-institutional and inter-institutional activities. The speed of light reduces many geographical barriers and the effects may be different in each of the four functions. The principal librarian must understand that which is best focused solely on the campus and that which must be "shared" with entities off the campus.

A conceptual structure for strategic planning for scholarly information, to this point, looks like the following:

- Human Resources
- Physical Resources
- Financial Resources
- Information Resources
    Scholarly Information
    Creation
    Collecting and Organizing
    Preserving and Storing
    Providing and Disseminating
        Inter-institutional
        Intra-institutional

A strategic plan addressing a five- and ten-year horizon for the university in the structure set forth above would provide a substantial step forward for the institution. It is important to note that the library organization has yet to appear in this context. We are focusing upon mission, resource, function, and method. Where the library, much less the computing center and the university press, performs its unique role is left to later stages of analysis. The point is to begin and then maintain sufficient momentum to continue.

Peter Drucker has written that we are in turbulent times that are "by definition . . . irregular, non-linear, erratic."[15] He suggests that there "are new realities, new opportunities, and new threats in the environment of . . . (the) institution."[16] New concepts of leadership, of management, and of strategic planning are needed to meet these turbulent times, for as Drucker continues:

> Planning starts out, as a rule, with the trends of yesterday and projects them into the future—using a different "mix" perhaps, but with very much the same elements and the same configuration. This is no longer going to work. The most probable assumption in a period of turbulence is the unique event which changes the configuration—and unique events cannot, by definition, be "planned." But they can often be foreseen. This requires strategies for tomorrow, strategies that

anticipate where the greatest changes are likely to occur and what they are likely to be, strategies that enable . . . a university (and a library)—to take advantage of new realities and to convert turbulence into opportunity.[17]

In this context, the actions that affect the university and the library the greatest may not be in its nature "but in its scale, rapidity, and coordination."[18] Put another way, the major dilemma of our modern times is "the disparity between our technology, on the one hand, with its rapid pace of advance and scope and, on the other, our institutional arrangements that are so slow to change and too often parochial in character."[19]

Finally, as Drucker notes, a "time of turbulence is also one of great opportunity for those who can understand, accept, and exploit the new realities. It is above all a time of opportunity for leadership."[20] Leaders who will guide their universities and their libraries on a way, especially by going in advance. Leaders with the courage to fail.

REFERENCES

1. John W. Gardner, *Self-Renewal, The Individual and the Innovative Society* (New York: Harper and Row, 1965), p. 14.

2. Gardner, p. 14.

3. Gardner, p. 15.

4. The Research Libraries Group, Inc., *1980: The Year in Review* (Stanford, CA: RLG, 1981).

5. John D. Millet, *Management, Governance and Leadership* (New York: AMACOM, 1980), p. 33.

6. Millet, pp. 36–37.

7. Millet, p. 40.

8. *Future Directions: Information Technology in Support of Scholarly and Administrative Activities*. Report of the Task Force on the Future of Computing (Stanford, CA: Stanford University, 1981), p. 30.

9. James Morris, *Heaven's Command, An Imperial Progress* (New York: Harvest/HBJ, 1980).

10. Private communication.

11. Victor C. Ferkiss, *Technological Man, The Myth and the Reality* (New York: New American Library, 1969), p. 208.

12. Ferkiss, p. 208.

13. Richard M. Lyman, *A Question of Leadership* (remarks at the Inauguration of the President of the University of Washington, 1974).

14. Millet, p. 21.

15. Peter F. Drucker, *Managing in Turbulent Times* (New York: Harper and Row, 1980), p. 2.

16. Drucker, p. 3.

17. Drucker, p. 4.

18. Daniel Bell, *The Coming of Post-Industrial Society* (New York: Basic Books, 1976), p. XVff.

19. George Ball, "Jean Monnet, A Modern Man for the Ages," *New York Times,* 20 March, 1979, editorial page.

20. Drucker, p. 5.

The Tool User

by Stephanie H. Stowe

It has been quite convincingly argued that the human race is at the end of its physical evolution and that what lies ahead is a mental evolution, the ramifications of which are as validly prophesied by the astrologer as by the biologist or the futurist.

Humans have already applied their facility with tools toward this evolutionary path by expanding their mental capabilities eternally (e.g., we created the computer). In doing so, we opened a Pandora's box, for we created the means not only for storing and communicating information but for generating additional information. As Branscomb indicates, "Information does not disintegrate when it is used: in fact, consumption generally increased its value."[1] It is the burgeoning of this information resource that leads Garfield to write of an "information society . . . in which we take for granted the role of information as it pervades and dominates the activities of government, business and everyday life"[2] and to project that 10 million terminals will be in use by 1989.

The advances in telecommunication and computer technologies will inexorably alter our future, affecting our social, economic, and political structures. We may be staggered by the thought of 130 million television sets connected to interactive systems, but the fact remains that this technology is already being tested in cities around the world. England's viewdata system Prestel can convey information from computer-accessed databases via telephone lines into slightly modified color television sets. According to Dew,

> Over 130 information providers contribute in collating reference material, news, information aids to management and services relating to vacancies and opportunities which are accessible from a simple terminal in the office. The same information services are available from terminals in homes together with services for consumer information, advice, educational aids and general travel information.[3]

By the year 2000, home terminals connected to office computers, teleconferencing, electronic publishing, and electronic mail will be everyday realities. Technology will permit an interconnecting of various types of information systems which will merge to form national, and later international, information pools. Sophisticated technologies such as audiovisual cassettes will be used for displaying information. High density storage on microform or other electromagnetic media will permit entire databases including text to be stored in minicomputers. The potentials for transmission are already innumerable: cable TV alone, which can be adapted as an interactive system, presently has a potential offering of 80 to 100 channels. Satellites such as CTS (Communications Technology Satellite) are currently used for data transmission. The potential uses of communication satellites for various library services are well-defined by Liu. Of greatest portent is the fact that three satellites can cover the principal inhabited regions of the earth. Additionally, transmission cost is independent of distance, response time is instantaneous (270 thousandths of a second), and reliable broadcast capabilities exist.[4]

Much as the gene pool of a species determined its evolutionary survival in the past, the use of the communal information pool of modern humans will determine the viability of their institutions, culture, and perhaps their future existence.

In discussing the role of leadership in special libraries through the year 2000, one is tempted to state that, if they survive, they have leaders. In a very real sense this is true, for special libraries are a diverse species. There is no single standard by which they are evaluated, and specialized services promoted in one institution may not be of equal value in another. Furthermore, their survival depends directly on their perceived benefits to the parent organization. If an organization should change its objectives by decreasing or eliminating research expenditures, the special library will be a line-item reduction.

Alma Wittlin wrote, "The first and main function of the public museum is to aid the adaptation of great masses of people to an environment characterized by an unprecedented rate of change in all conditions of life."[5] The analogous function of the special library is to aid its parent organization in adapting to change. This is both a valid and critical function. It was a belief in the validity of this function fused with a philosophical attitude toward serving the public which made John Cotton Dana an innovative and effective leader in both the museum and library worlds. As one of the original founders, and the first president of the Special Libraries Association, Dana was instrumental in developing the concept of service to business people. Creatively building a very unorthodox, utilitarian collection of business literature (trade catalogs, government documents, statistics, maps) at the Newark Public Library, Dana found that business people might not be persuaded to read books, but they could be persuaded to use them.

Developing collections and services in anticipation of and in response to user needs has continued to be intrinsic to special library development.

Halm states that "the main difference between a special library and other types of libraries, seems to be in its user-oriented access."[6] It is this user-oriented access which has validated the past development of special libraries in government, business, and industry and which will be the key to their continuance in the future. However, "as the complexity of the immediate organizational environment and the larger social environment increases and intensifies, the librarian's need for data on pertinent trends and likely developments inside and outside the parent institution increases."[7]

Ladendorf has suggested that the special library should be functioning as one of the major adaptive units within the organization. An adaptive unit is one which is deeply concerned with the world outside of organizational boundaries; it studies this world to determine what changes may be necessary either within the organization or in the outside world in order to ensure the organization's continuing survival.[8] It may be that the trends monitored by the library will provide critical decision-making data for corporate and institutional actions.

The skills for the requisite monitoring and action outlined in the foregoing will demand a high level of creativity: creativity which challenges assumptions; makes connections between seemingly unrelated tasks, services, and technologies to accommodate users; and takes the risks necessary to implement new technologies and services. The essence of creativity is the capacity to bear and even enjoy extended uncertainty.[9]

The future will also demand that special librarians become generalists, capable of assessing the complex factors which have an impact on any corporate manager and of initiating appropriate responses. Although one is hesitant to differentiate between a special librarian and an information specialist, the generalist of the future will have broader information responsibilities, including activities such as editing, publishing, research synthesis, records management, and data generation.

Although special librarians serving multinational corporations and agencies have had a "global perspective" from their inception, most special libraries have perceived their organization in relationship to local, regional, and national affairs. Increasingly, international affairs will affect the actions of U.S. corporations and institutions, and the special librarian will be expected to provide timely, accurate data on trends abroad.

The social responsibility of librarians has been defined as "the relationships that librarians and libraries have to nonlibrary problems that relate to the social welfare of our society."[10] Concerns such as privacy, censorship, fair use, and intellectual freedom will continue to be foci of controversy. Shields discusses an extemely critical social issue which should be of concern to all librarians:

> Today we are faced with a society dependent upon its technology. We are faced with a technology which thrives on acceleration. And with that acceleration goes social change. And if society cannot find the information it needs to know to meet the accelerated pace of decision-making, then technology becomes destructive rather than constructive. And in a destructive society, information falls into the hands of a few.[11]

In 1979, the Information Industry Association estimated that only one-sixth of the population of the United States was informationally literate or had the skill and knowledge to use information tools to effect solutions to problems.

The new technologies capable of transmitting vast amounts of information may be the causal agents of "electromagnetic pollution." Here, the special librarian with a strong subject background will perform a significant function in filtering and synthesizing relevant information. Additionally, while it is expected that commercial information systems will continue to develop natural language programs to facilitate direct user interaction, guidance in determining the appropriate ones for searching will be needed. This will be especially important in evaluating potential usefulness of nonbibliographic databases.

With the foregoing comments in mind, it is obvious that, while future special librarians will continue to assume an active role in developing and/or expanding information transfer systems appropriate to the needs of their users, the success of these systems will be highly dependent on the successful use of electronic technologies.

The use of computer-based systems is not new to special libraries. In the mid-60s, the necessity of providing highly customized services with limited resources forced many special libraries into creating and using computer-based systems before other libraries recognized the potential of the technology.[12] Lockheed's DIALOG system was developed to provide access to 200,000 NASA citations. Highly sophisticated systems such as MEDLARS, later to become MEDLINE, and internally created systems adequately filled user needs; however, a broadening of perspectives nationally combined with economic necessity has resulted in the entrance of special libraries into formal networking. Budgetary constraints will undoubtedly intensify resource-sharing efforts until such time as electronic document delivery systems are perfected.

The addition of special library records to online technical support systems such as OCLC, RLIN, UTLAS, and state systems greatly enhances the depth and usefulness of these systems. Computerized technical functions which have application to individual special libraries, or to special libraries as part of networks, include cataloging, location, verification, collection development, serials control, circulation, acquisitions, local databases, and subject searching.

Online commercial bibliographic databases of Lockheed have expanded to over 100, serving thousands of users in 40 countries. As of December 1979, nine online vendors offered over 130 bibliographic databases in science and technology alone.[13] It is expected that the phenomenal growth of databases will continue, enhancing the special librarian's ability to meet specific information requests and to provide access to materials peripheral to the library's subject specialty. However, coverage duplication and lack of standardization in file construction, to say nothing of hardware standardization, will create innumerable complications affecting searching.

Nonbibliographic databases will become increasingly important to special library users. Over 400 databases are available online, and the majority of these are nonbibliographical. The nonbibliographic area encompasses a number of different types of databases, including referral, numeric, textual-numeric, chemical and physical properties, and full-text.[14] Creatively used, these data banks are extremely powerful information tools for they permit integration and manipulation of the user's own data with data gathered by government agencies (e.g., census reports) and/or by the private sector (e.g., public survey findings).

The linking of bibliographic with nonbibliographic databases will be an extremely valuable accomplishment in the next decade. Structure and Nomenclature Search System (SANSS), which is constructed to allow chemical compounds to be identified by full or partial name or structure, can be connected to CA SEARCH with registry numbers retrieving appropriate bibliographic citations.

Multitype library communication links are also being developed rapidly. In Colorado, the ORACLE (a dial-up experimental telephone network) provides online computer messages and data communication to special, public, and academic libraries. The menu includes event calendars, jobline, interlibrary loan, conferencing option, and article submittal and access to the newsletters of the Colorado ORACLE computer via any standard telephone line from anywhere in the world.

Integrating and standardizing these systems will be one of the greatest challenges facing the special librarian and other librarians in the next 20 years.

By the year 2000, special librarians will have participated in the development of systems which will be able to search the holdings of other libraries/information centers through networks, to access bibliographic and nonbibliographic databases, to transmit and receive documents electronically, to create internal files, and to generate appropriate data from them.

While society prefers to judge the abilities of members of a profession in relation to the ''leaders'' of that profession, new niches in the rapidly changing environment are filled by adaptable species. It is perhaps in retrospect only that we will be able to look at the years between 1980 and 2000 and distinguish those individuals who made outstanding contributions to the profession. Whether or not they are recognized in their own time is probably immaterial in this age of rapid information transfer, for innovative technologies and services which enhance user-oriented services will be readily transmitted, adapted, and employed. The originator of the idea may never be discerned.

The diversity of special libraries now in existence reflects the nature of our nation and its multitude of constituencies. Special librarians are found in financial, commercial, industrial, governmental, and nonprofit organizations, such as local, state, and federal agencies, banks, research labs, insurance companies, planning firms, newspapers, law firms, manufacturing companies, museums, exploration companies, and special collections which are part of larger collections.

Although the individual qualities discussed currently appear to be relevant to special librarians in the year 2000, it is perhaps unrealistic, and even detrimental, to look for one leader or a small group of leaders to appear in an era which demands such a high level of flexibility and creativity, and in a profession serving a myriad of institutional goals. That outstanding individual leaders are not predicted for the special library field may be of concern to some readers; however, as Kissinger suggests: ''A society that must produce a great man in each generation to maintain its domestic or international position will doom itself.''[15]

One is more inclined to prophesize advancements in the special library field through the connection of many individual achievements which will gain value as they interact with each other, much as Branscomb suggests that the use of information increases its value. The majority of achievements will involve innovative applications of our electronic tools; however, of ultimate consequence will be the wisdom with which we use our tool-generated information.

REFERENCES

1. Lewis M. Branscomb, ''Information: The Ultimate Frontier,'' *Science* 203 (1979): 143–47.

2. Eugene Garfield, ''2001: An Information Society,'' *Journal of Information Science* 1 (1979): 209–15.

3. Bryan Dew, "The Prestel System and Information Retrieval," *Program* 14 (1980): 76–89.

4. Rosa Liu, "Telelibrary: Library Services via Satellite," *Special Libraries* 70 (1979): 363–72.

5. Alma S. Wittlin, *The Museum: Its History and Its Tasks in Education* (London: Routledge and Kegan Paul, 1949), p. 297.

6. Johan van Halm, *The Development of Special Libraries as an International Phenomena* (New York: Special Libraries Association, 1978), p. 626.

7. Miriam A. Drake, "The Environment for Special Libraries in the 1980s," *Special Libraries* 71 (1980): 509–18.

8. Janice M. Ladendorf, "The Special Librarian in the Modern World," *Special Libraries* 61 (1970): 531–37.

9. Ladendorf, pp. 531–37.

10. Arthur Curley, "Social Responsibilities and Libraries," *Advances in Librarianship,* vol. 4 (New York: Academic Press, 1974), p. 78.

11. Gerald R. Shields, "The New Role of Librarian," *The Information Society: Issues and Answers,* ed. E. J. Josey (Phoenix, AZ: Oryx Press, 1978), p. 133.

12. Mary Ellen Jacob, Ann T. Dodson, and Nancy Fennigan, "Special Libraries and Databases: A State-of-the-Art Report," *Special Libraries* 72 (1981): 103–12.

13. John J. Regazzi, Bruce Bennion, and Susan Roberts, "On-line Systems of Disciplines and Speciality Areas in Science and Technology," *Journal of the Society for Information Science* 31 (1980): 161–80.

14. Judith Wagner and Ruth N. Landau, "Nonbibliographic On-Line Date Base Services," *Journal of the American Society for Information Science* 31 (1980): 171–80.

15. "In Quest of Leadership," *Time* 104 (1974): 21–34.

A Good Heart and an Organized Mind: Leadership in Technical Services

by Michael Gorman

Reason and judgment are the qualities of a leader. *Tacitus*

The Chinese are reputed to curse their enemies by saying, "May you live in interesting times." These are interesting times in the area of technical services. Though the term "technical services" has a variety of interpretations, it stands in the minds of most as the activities associated with the processing of books and other materials in libraries. These activities commonly encompass acquisition, cataloging, serial control, maintenance of paper files and machine-readable databases, and binding. More than any other area of librarianship, technical services has been influenced by the two dominant forces which act on modern librarianship—economics and automation. We are constantly seeking ways to cope with monetary shortages without harming the more obvious forms of reader service; we seek ways of processing more with less by using automation effectively; and we seek to use computers to improve simultaneously the speed and quality of our processing and our cost-effectiveness. These are no small tasks. The anonymous and largely misunderstood toilers in the technical services vineyards are suffering from a crisis that is, at least partly, psychological. Lacking the visibility of those who have personal contact with the users of the library, often hearing only negative comments, and struggling with a continuously renewing problem, there is small wonder that technical services staffs feel themselves undervalued, directionless, and in great need of leadership. Tragically, that leadership is often not there.

The great law of culture—let each become all that he was
created capable of being. *Thomas Carlyle*

What is the true watchword of leadership? *Be what you want to become*.
If we are to create libraries which respond effectively to the challenge of, and

the possibilities raised by, the era of limits and of automation, we have to have a clear idea of what those libraries should be like and we have to be daring enough to make our libraries conform to that future ideal.

There is a range of possible reactions to the need to work within a restricted budget and the desire to take advantage of automation. At one end of the range, we find leadership. The rest of the range consists of, at best, management and, at worst, incompetence and insulation from reality. In this essay, I wish to analyze the differences between these various responses, to define the nature of leadership as contrasted with administration and management, and to propose an agenda for the leader in technical services for the years to come.

The essential differences between management/administration on the one hand and leadership on the other is that the former is concerned with what is and the latter is concerned with what will be. One accepts the *status quo* (and often yearns for the *status quo ante*); the other dares to imagine and to create the future. In technical services, the manager/administrator strives to make the returns of the current system as great as possible, whereas the leader seeks better alternatives to the current system. One wishes for changes which are different in kind. The case of the introduction of the OCLC system in our libraries is one very common and crucial example of the shortcomings of the approach taken by the manager/administrator. The typical pattern of behavior of heads of technical services was to mandate or to allow the control of OCLC by already established cataloging departments. In almost every case, the system and its most obvious manifestation (the OCLC terminals) were not used to their capacity because their real value and the change which they represent were not understood. Cataloging departments saw the terminals, when they saw them as anything other than a threat, as devices to enable them to continue their present practices. In sum, OCLC was generally seen as being of marginal benefit and as an essentially conservative force, making existing systems better without changing the nature of those systems. Managers/administrators noted a small increase in cataloging productivity and believed the innovation to be successful. The truth was quite otherwise.

The true role of leadership lies in anticipating the future, in understanding the impact of new technologies, and in making adjustments in organizational patterns to meet both the demands of the future and the needs of technical services personnel. In this last role lies another vital attribute of the leader: the ability to sense, articulate, and respond to the needs of the library's employees (professional, paraprofessional, and nonprofessional) and always to accept them as human beings with professional and personal aspirations that are more important than the corporate aims of the library. Not the least reason for this attitude is that any institution which seeks to elevate its corporate concerns over those of the individuals who make up the library staff will undoubtedly fail in that endeavor. There are practical, as well as moral, reasons behind the need for a leader to have a good heart as well as an organized mind.

The world of technical services has changed to an extent almost unimaginable one or two decades ago. One common fault of technical services administrators is always to regard these changes as having a negative effect on the working lives of the personnel. It is true that technical processing provides employment for fewer persons than in the past, and that trend will probably persist. On the other hand, those persons still employed in technical processing are almost invariably engaged in more fulfilling and effective tasks. The ability to articulate the advantages, as well as the disadvantages of change, is an important part of the quality of leadership.

We are faced, in technical services, with doing more with less. At the same time as we have to absorb the disproportionate amount of the budget cuts (in real dollars) that face almost every library, we are also required to obtain and process materials more quickly than in the past, to create new and better systems of bibliographic control (notably new and better catalogs), and to respond to changes in technology that are more extensive than those in any other area of librarianship.

No one believes that the old attitudes and the old structures of technical services are adequate to fulfill these tremendous and often conflicting obligations. There are two responses, broadly speaking. The first, and regrettably the most common, reaction is to proceed in a fashion one might describe as that of the manager, which is typified by the lack of a long-range strategy, by a type of nostalgia, and by a quiescence that avoids prediction and concentrates on the exigencies of the present. The second response, that of a leader, is characterized by an acceptance of the implications of change, by a desire to progress, and by a comprehensive strategy that rejects the constriction of the past.

The strategy of the leader in a time of change can be summed as consisting of: (1) a willingness to adapt the organization of technical services; (2) a desire and an ability to rationalize; (3) an acceptance of automation and its implications; and (4) a desire to engage in useful and realistic cooperation.

I do not see these four elements as being either consecutive or discrete; rather, they are interconnected elements of an overall strategy and each depends on and illuminates the others. Each of these elements is essential to leadership in technical services today, and each, especially the last, demonstrates an awareness of the context of technical services (i.e., an ability to see beyond the mere procedures of processing and to escape the preoccupation with means and obliviousness to ends which have bedevilled most of librarianship in the past).

We must reform if we would conserve.   *Franklin Delano Roosevelt*

The first element in the strategy of the leader (that of reorganization) is the most concrete and often the most politically complicated undertaking that faces the leader. It may be personally hazardous to him/her. There are a few people in any walk of life (and probably fewer in librarianship than in most vocations) who welcome change in the structures and routines of their working days. There is a definite danger that the leader may be compromised in the eyes of technical services personnel by an even slightly misjudged or mishandled reorganization plan. There is the virtual certainty that any reorganization (no matter how well-conceived and executed) will leave a residue of disaffected and embittered individuals who believe that their personal status has been damaged or annihilated in the process of change. With all these hazards and difficulties, why is reorganization worth doing?

I believe that in all, or almost all, technical services operations there is a clear and present need to reorganize and clear benefits to be gained by doing so. In great part, this need and these benefits arise from the fact that changing times call for changing structures to accommodate them. No one disputes the fact that the times have changed drastically for libraries in general and for processing in particular. Any organizational structure which is, in its essentials, more than 20 years old was devised to cope with a library environment that has been utterly changed. Bibliographic networks, OCLC's electronic union catalog, AACR2, MARC, automated circulation and other short record systems, automated serial control, multitype library resource-sharing systems, and vendors of library materials with sophisticated computer systems were merely dreamed of, or unthought of, 20 years ago. Over the same period, the Farmington Plan, micro-opaques, printed serial union lists, edge-notched and peek-a-boo cards, LC proof slips, NPAC, and the ALA Cataloging Rules of 1949 have either become one with Nineveh and Tyre or are the playthings of a few backward-looking librarians. All this change has been focused by the cruel light of the seemingly unending budget crunch. Most of our staffing patterns and organizational structures have changed little or not at all despite the fact that the very essence of the tasks for which those patterns and structures were designed has been transformed. Structures that respond to present realities are of the first importance to modern technical processing. It is the task of the leader to conceive and create those structures. This task requires a certainty of purpose and a resolution that springs from a reasonable self-confidence.

It is not entirely facetious to suggest that *any* reorganization is good for the library. The germ of truth which lies in this assertion is that any reorganization provokes a reassessment of procedures and patterns and that such a reassessment must, of its nature, be useful. That reassessment or analysis of the present state of technical processing is an essential first step.

Even a simple procedure, such as flowcharting the work in technical processing (a necessary precondition of reorganization), can be most informative. When an organized mind is brought to bear on such charts, weaknesses and illogicalities become evident. The things to look for are duplications of effort, lack of communication of information, and unnecessary elaborations in the flow of materials or the construction of files. This simple first step provides the basis for analysis. What should that analysis be directed towards? It should be concentrated upon the variables of speed, quality, efficiency, and cost-effectiveness and towards the product of their totality which is service. The analyst will do well to remember the Shavian maxim: *Never accept*. By this, I mean that no pattern, no process, no file should be left unchallenged by the process of analysis. The analysis is a relatively objective stage and a relatively easy state for the leader. The stage of reorganization and modification of the processes described in the analysis is not so easy. There is certainly no need to assume that rigid hierarchies are inevitable or desirable. Libraries and their processing departments, though they share certain grand generalities of aim with others, vary widely in the specifics of their purposes. I believe that there is, however, one main theme of organization which does apply to all processing operations. It is that most modern technical processing operations will do well to organize around their functions rather than around the type of material with which they deal. Economy and logic are both better served if, for example, all ordering, claiming, and receiving are concentrated in one organizational division. The maintenance of order files, the control of payment, the maintenance of blanket order and approval plans, the claiming of overdue orders are best done in an integrated manner. The perceived advantages of arranging for such a function to be carried out in a variety of disparate units with differing functions are, in my findings, far outweighed by the inefficiencies and duplicate procedures which such arrangements inevitably engender. I would stress that the theme of integration of functions is not immutable. The changes and technologies of the next 20 years may well make the theme obsolete. In this, as everywhere else, we see the necessity for a leader who can not only respond to the needs of today but can also remain open to the implications of change in a continuing manner. One can never assume that the right answer to a problem is the right answer for all time. This flexibility of approach and willingness to reconsider are both important qualities for anyone who wishes to lead.

He who will not reason is a bigot; he who cannot is a fool;
and he who dares not is a slave. *Thomas Drummond*

With the difficult problem of reorganization overcome, the leader needs to concentrate on the other parts of the agenda I have outlined. Rationalization is, of course, a component of reorganization and depends to some extend on the automation and cooperation which I will discuss later. Although there is a definite place for creativity and flair in the makeup of the leader in this field, I believe that a determinedly rational approach to technical processing (i.e., the organized mind mentioned in the title of this essay) is the most important intellectual attribute for a leader. The ability to distinguish between form and substance, to analyze procedures with a view to improving them, and to have a grasp of the logical process are all vital to success in technical processing. When these are allied with a questioning approach, the leader has formidable advantages.

I would illustrate rationalization and the benefits which it can bring by describing what I call the drift down of responsibility. Logic dictates that any task should be performed at the lowest level at which it can be accomplished successfully. In technical processing, this means that no professional should do a task which a paraprofessional can do, no paraprofessional should do a task which a clerical assistant can do, and no person should do a job which a machine can do. In traditional technical processing, these strata of responsibility have been mixed and muddled up together. I would cite the examples of professionals doing copy cataloging, routine order verification, or simple classification and Cuttering, all to the detriment of the time spent on truly professional tasks. This muddle has extended to the point at which, in many technical services areas, there is a form of identity crisis in which professional librarians doubt their professional worth and escape into the clerical routines in which they feel comfortable. Rationalization can cure this problem, as well as making the library more efficient and cost effective. A manger could well come to the conclusion that it is inefficient and uneconomic to pay relatively highly paid professionals to do tasks which could be accomplished for half the money. I submit that it takes a leader to recognize that beyond the economics lie some human problems which, if resolved, will benefit the library in ways that transcend the saving of money. Librarians doing professional work have more self-esteem and more involvement. This must benefit the library. Paraprofessionals and clerical staff who are, on the one hand, given tasks which carry more responsibility and, on the other hand, relieved of drudgery by automation, will almost inevitably perform better and feel happier. It is reason that will lead to this outcome, but it is human sensitivity that informs the process and creates the most benefit to individuals and the library. One can be a manager with an organized mind. One can be a decent human being with a good heart. One needs both to be a leader. The restructuring or drift down of authority is but one example of the benefits of rationalization. A rational approach to other problems will always bring similar benefits.

> During my eighty-seven years I have witnessed a whole
> succession of technological revolutions. None has done away with the
> need for character in the individual or the need to think.
>
> *Bernard Baruch*

An intensely practical problem facing the leader in today's library is one's approach to automation. The question is not whether to automate (that has been disposed of to the satisfaction of all but a few mossbacks) but how to automate. More precisely, the question is how to take advantage of the numerous benefits of automation. Although the range of responses to automation has narrowed from the time when it ran from futuristic euphoria to acute fear, there are still human and attitudinal problems in achieving the benefits of automation. Therefore, in approaching the question of the role of automation in one's library, one cannot rely solely on practical and economic criteria. This human problem is, happily, shown by experience to be transient. Anyone who has tried to persuade a person in an automated part of the library to revert to working in a nonautomated division will know that, when it comes to terminals, old habits die easily and that personnel soon discover the manifest advantages to them of working with a machine system. Opposition to automation by library staff and library patrons is, I am convinced, a matter of ignorance breeding fear. The leader will take care to inform, to demonstrate and, thus, to dispel the clouds of unreason.

In practical terms, there are a number of ways in which libraries can participate in the benefits of automation. They can install their own systems; they can participate in established systems; they can establish new systems in collaboration with others; and they can pay for automated services provided by commercial vendors. Inevitably, libraries will come up with a mix of these various options. The library in which I work is a member and heavy user of OCLC. We have our own circulation and short-record system; we are participating in a successful statewide endeavor to extend the latter system to a number of libraries; and we subscribe to a serial vendor with an advanced automated system. There is a danger in this approach. It is that the necessities and tactics of this piecemeal participation will obscure or eliminate the long-term strategic goals of the library. Here, the role of the leader is pivotal. Only someone with a broad view of the future and of the ultimate aims of the library can judge each move into automation and fit it into the grand design. Failure to do this will not become apparent for a number of years—years in which short-term goals will be achieved at the expense of the long-term effectiveness and utility of the library.

The key example for the future of automation is the achievement of the online catalog. Though such a catalog has yet to be established in a general library of any size, its makeup and capabilities are generally agreed. The online catalog poses a unique set of political, economic, technical, and professional problems to the leader seeking to establish such a system. On the political level, there are the following considerations: (1) institutional acceptance of major change; (2) patron acceptance of major change; (3) public and technical services staff acceptance of major change; and (4) for public institutions, added dimensions of municipal, state, or regional acceptance of major change.

These complex political problems test the personal qualities of the leader. S/he needs a sensitivity to the web of relationships among these various groups, an ability to articulate the advantages of the future system, and a political savvy of a high order. Much will depend on existing personal and institutional relationships, and a true leader will have taken care to build and cultivate these. In such a public relations and political exercise, the belief and commitment of the leader must be evident. In other words, successful leadership here, as elsewhere, involves a true and manifest sense of purpose.

On the economic level, the inevitable initial capital expenditure has to be obtained and set against long-term financial gains. Only with success on the political level can such capital funds be sought successfully. Much of the money, of course, can be spent either on devising, constructing, and installing a "home-made" system or on purchasing, modifying, and installing existing software. I strongly believe that, almost without exception, libraries will be wise to purchase and adapt existing systems. The development of advanced computer-based bibliographic systems consumes a great deal of money and, perhaps more importantly, demands a large amount of human resources which are often not available. In addition, replication of existing systems offers possibilities for future cooperation and interaction and is, thus, more progressive than the construction of inward-looking "uncommunicative" local systems. In either event, additional funds or resources will be needed to sustain the operating system, its computers, and its terminal network. The analysis of the defects of existing card or other linear form catalogs which will precede a change to online systems will show clearly that the change can be justifed on both long-term economic and increased service grounds. These two benefits should be clearly distinguished and their long-term nature should be understood and stressed. It is easy to fall into the trap of raising expectations too high in terms of both time and benefit. People readily expect too much too soon. It is prudent administration to do one's sums correctly. It is the task of leadership to understand and explain the implications of financial computations and to relate them to the benefits to be derived. In this, as in other areas, the leader goes beyond considerations of cost-effectiveness to the more important and more difficult considerations of cost-benefit.

The technical and professional problems involved in the establishment of the online catalog are considerable and require a variety of kinds of expertise. The leader should recognize the expertise that is required and assemble a team of individuals with the necessary skills. His/her task in this respect is to indicate the directions that the project should take, to devise a structure which will enable the individuals in the team to interact fruitfully, to monitor the progress of the project, and, when necessary, to make adjustments to the project. This team approach is an essential element in the success of an online catalog project. The ability of the leader to assemble, inspire, and direct such a team is not the least of his/her attributes.

I have dwelled on the problems and challenges of the online catalog because I believe that this topic best illustrates the many aptitudes required of the leader in the technical services field. The ability to reason, personal and professional qualities, and administrative and inspirational skills are called for if such a project is to succeed.

> The alternative to the totalitarian state is the cooperative
> commonwealth. *Norman Thomas*

The last element of the agenda for the leader in technical services is that of cooperation. I use this term not only in its usual sense of positive interaction between libraries but also in two other senses: cooperation between technical and public services departments and cooperation between the leader and the staff of technical services.

A positive and cooperative approach to the problems of technical services which involves all the kinds and levels of staff is an essential element of success. In my conception, leadership does not imply authoritarianism. The authoritarian is someone who cannot, or will not, convince and inspire his/her fellow workers. If one cannot inspire by example and by the force of one's ideas, one has no business being a leader. If one can do this but does not trouble to, one lacks an attribute of crucial importance, which is the concern for the integrity and feelings of one's colleagues. Authoritarianism is a philosophy of cowardice in which one lacks the courage to articulate and defend one's ideas. It is also sterile because, without such articulation and defense, those ideas are neither refined nor improved. The true leader believes in his/her ideas and has confidence in his/her abilities. S/he does not feel threatened by discussion or criticism. The true leader does not believe that position implies superiority or that the power of position should be used irresponsibly. In escaping from the rigid hierarchies of the old organization of libraries, one is freeing not only those who were oppressed by such hierarchies but also those who dominated them. The true leader recognizes that, in an effective library department, all persons are valued for the particular skills or attributes they bring to their tasks. A skillful terminal operator is to be as valued as a good systems analyst or an effective senior administrator. Once the technical service group members have broken through to this realization, they are in a position to work in a positive way as colleagues and not as inferiors and superiors. The practical effort of this realization is that new methods need to be employed so that library personnel can feel themselves to be valued, can communicate in a multidimensional framework, and can feel themselves to be informed and trusted. None of these desirable consequences are easy to achieve because old patterns of behavior leave their stamp on individuals and groups. The leader should demonstrate belief in a system of values and trust and devise mechanisms for cooperative achievement in which s/he is not a dictator but a focus, not an authoritarian but a democrat.

Having established a new sense of cooperation in technical services, the leader should attempt to establish cooperation between the parts of the library. The destructive effect of the dichotomy between "public" and "technical" services is still not widely recognized. It is, however, a fact. As long as these groups each claim uniqueness in library service, as long as one is seen as being less important than the other, and as long as we accept the implication that librarianship as a profession and library work as a service lack wholeness, we will suffer and our library users will suffer. Librarianship and the library must be seen as a whole. They compose a complex system dedicated to the preservation of knowledge and great cultural values and to service to all who seek information, knowledge, and culture in all fields. The task of breaking down entrenched attitudes of superiority and defensiveness is not light. The leader in technical services must persevere because, without that integration of the strands of librarianship, no one element can be truly effective. The leader must be prepared to suffer rebuffs in this attempt and must constantly seek new structures for the new integrated librarianship.

Cooperation between libraries has been much talked about for many years. The "fortress library" mentality is still with us though, mercifully, weaker than it has ever been. It is sad, but true, that the present striving for more cooperation is a product of hard economic times. Libraries are being forced into resource sharing, cooperative acquisition, and cooperative cataloging because they can no longer afford to acquire everything they need and to catalog their acquisitions themselves. This is unfortunate because cooperation has a much wider and nobler aim—the bringing of library resources to all who need them. Cooperation should imply an escape from parochialism, an end to elitist concepts, and a desire to benefit everyone regardless of their institutional affiliation. The leader in technical services must be aware of this larger purpose and must place each advance in technique into a wider context. For example, the question of whether a large research library should use OCLC or the Research Libraries Group (RLIN) project can readily be resolved on financial and practical grounds. However, there are higher grounds. A desire to cooperate and to bring the benefits of library resources to all will inevitably lead to a preference for the comprehensive system over the elitist group.

Cooperation with other libraries has many consequences for technical processing. Some are entirely benign and some present difficulties. The leader in technical processing will weigh those consequences carefully and will take care to ensure that each move in the technical services area is looked at in the light of the cooperative ideals and realities.

CONCLUSION

The leader in technical services combines administrative skills (an organized mind) with personal sensitivity (a good heart). S/he must be competent without being mechanistic, must be visionary and idealistic without being wooly-minded, and must be a leader without being power hungry. S/he must be aware of the complexities of the many contexts in which technical services work is carried out. The leader is a wo/man of character, intelligence, human sympathy, and purpose. These are exacting criteria and few, or none of us, match them all. They do, however, set our goals and help us to define the nature of our work and responsibilities. If we tackle our many duties and problems with a good heart and an organized mind, we shall inevitably prevail.

Information Is Power:
The Future of Collection
Development in Libraries

by Dora Biblarz

Life in the latter part of the twentieth century is certainly more complex than anyone would have been able to predict 20 years ago. It seems that, in the United States, the aftermath of protest and free speech movements, followed by the Vietnam War, has left a demoralizing effect on the population. The decade of the 70s can be characterized by a condition that undermines the benefits of progress: inflation. The results are becoming clear. We are in a period of economic uncertainty; political conservatism, as well as extremism; and disappointment with the realization that the ''good life'' is not, as formerly thought, achievable by everyone.

Another phenomenon that we face, the ramifications of which are yet to be fully determined, is the shift of the centers of population in the United States. As the older, more established cities of the northeast are abandoned for the sunbelt, publicly supported institutions stagger under diminished resources and the effects of inflation. On the other hand, the emerging centers of urban population cannot cope quickly enough with the change and the impact of exponentially increased demands on their services.

The next two decades will be filled with continued uncertainty, as we assess the impact of inflation which still plagues us and saps our diminishing resources. We are in a period of transition, entering an age where sophisticated electronic technology could present some solutions to our present problems. If our culture is to survive, we need leaders who will help solve the problems by guiding us through the necessary changes.

Educational institutions, whether public or private, are being hit hard by all the problems of the economy. In addition, the declining birth rate in this country is resulting in a higher median age, thus changing the profile of the traditional student.

The picture, as it focuses on libraries, looks bleak indeed. Libraries that are associated with publicly supported institutions have to struggle for survival alongside their parent organizations in vying for taxpayer support. Privately funded libraries are also required to demonstrate their utility in order to successfully compete for funding. Few, if any, service-oriented institutions will survive the next two decades unless their user clientele is fully satisfied. Without certain changes in priorities and, in some cases, radically different responsiveness to the demands of their users, some services will not survive the next two decades.

Regardless of the sources of funding, libraries in the next 20 years will be required to make certain choices: Will they focus their reason for being on their role as museums of the printed word or will they become information brokers? Certainly, some libraries, or parts of libraries, will be needed to fulfill the archival goal of society to preserve books and other printed information for posterity. However, if libraries expect to survive and prosper in a dynamic way, they will need to focus on their immediate goal as providers of information.

As we advance technologically, the amount of information generated increases by quantum leaps. Printed forms of storage are becoming more expensive to produce, acquire, and preserve, while the complexity of access makes their contents almost irretrievable. But, information is power and the key to success in any endeavor. Libraries which can effectively provide the information needed, without regard to the storage medium, will be successful. The next 20 years will be a period of transition for libraries from their current identity as museum collections to a new outlook as information brokers; collection development personnel will be the change agents.

What is meant by collection development? No matter what the setting, collection development is the deliberate addition and deletion of pieces which share some common factor in harmony with a stated goal. One can develop a collection of seashells or the works of Salvador Dali. The goal of the collection may be comprehensiveness, that is, every piece executed by Dali, or selectivity by some factor, such as shells only from the Pacific Ocean. Here, we will be concerned only with collections of recorded information: for example, popular fiction, results of current research in nuclear physics, or folk songs and traditional dances of the Navajo.

These collections are brought together for a specific purpose, funded directly or indirectly by the population of users. There is generally an institution associated with these collections, and the goals of the collection conform to the philosophy of the institution. The groups of potential users have certain common characteristics and some common expectations from the collections.

The deliberate addition and deletion of pieces of recorded information which are gathered in pursuit of a common goal, and in conformity with the philosophy of the parent institution, constitute collection development. The location of this information will be referred to as a library, although it may be more than the physical location for a collection. By the year 2000, a library will collect information recorded on microform, audio cassettes, and magnetic tape, in addition to the latest technologically advanced storage media, such as laser discs, videotapes, and means we haven't even thought of yet. A library in 20 years will have much more than its own collection at the command of its users, for access through electronic means will make available other collections to complement local holdings.

The institutions with which the library is affiliated need not be in the business of education, but the educational needs of its users are usually objectives that libraries seek to fulfill. In the coming years, as information of a highly specialized nature proliferates, many more special libraries will develop for the use of associations, industries, businesses, and professional groups. The collection, in some cases, may only consist of the documents or archives of the institution, but it is still likely to fit into the broad definitions stated here. Public libraries will probably need to take innovative approaches to the philosophical foundations of their collections in order to successfully compete for the support of the taxpayers.

Libraries will not be able to achieve and retain the high priority needed to function, as well as grow, unless they can justify their existence to the satisfaction of their particular source of funding. The type and amount of support received will continue to be affected by the service and quality of information received by the users. The collection, by either direct or remote access, will be the source of the information sought by the user, thereby linking directly the goal with the end result. There will undoubtedly continue to be a need for an intermediary interpreter or expediter for the use of the collection, since the variety of formats containing recorded information will most likely not be uniformly accessible.

The librarian or archivist will continue to act as the expediter of access to the recorded information in the collection. Ideally, this would be the same person as the one responsible for the development of the collection, but, if not, there should be some method of communication between the librarian-interpreter and the collector. In some collections, there will be only one person who is responsible for everything; this simplifies collection-related decisions. The staff members who make selection and other collection development-related decisions will be referred to as selectors, regardless of other duties.

Leaders in the area of collection development will be seeking solutions to the problems that confront libraries today, in addition to those of the institution with which the library is affiliated. Their most important role will be to build and shape a collection of information which responds to the needs of the users and conforms to the stated philosophy and goals of the parent institution.

The first priority in preparation for the future is the statement of guiding principles for the collection. This statement is ideally based on the mission and goals of the library and the institution with which it is affiliated. It contains guidelines for the selectors which define the borders of the collection; it becomes the "road map" of the collection. In such a statement, the user or the interpreter should be able to find, in general terms, if the information sought can be located in the collection. Before looking for specific titles or subjects, the user should find out at a glance whether or not the desired item is in a category that is available directly or if the material is accessible only in the resources of another library.

In the past, collection guidelines have not been given a high priority in libraries, partly because they are difficult to articulate in specific terms and meaningless if stated in general terms. On the other hand, libraries in the past had a finite universe of recorded information to cope with. Today, and in the next two decades, our society needs to contend with an increasingly large amount of information which conforms to few criteria regarding medium or format. Finally, while research libraries of a major significance were built in the past by the collection efforts of a single individual, we need to develop techniques for the future that no longer depend on unique people with renaissance tastes. Dowd elaborates on the urgency of the need for a collection development policy statement and suggests an excellent methodology for writing one.[1]

Whatever the degree of complexity of the collection, it is important to find an accurate and flexible way to describe the collection and the objectives that guide its shaping. Without such a document, the evaluation of the success or failure of the collection and its value as a major investment cannot take place.

Collections with primary goals oriented to the provision of information will incorporate into their policy statements the limits, as well as the depth and breadth, of their collection efforts. Having in mind the ultimate goal of providing access to information for the user, the guidelines will refer to regional or national resources (even international, eventually) which supplement the materials available locally.

The creation of such an abundance of information must be followed by a method of managing it. Automation of this, like many other processes related to the organization of the library, is the only effective way to control it and keep it current. While automation still provides the only alternative for moving libraries through the turbulent final decades of the twentieth century, the process will be cumbersome and expensive, as De Gennaro points out.[2] The investment in a library quickly changes from costly to nearly unreasonable. Collections need to be acquired, processed, stored, and retrieved, and this has to become a much more streamlined, cost-effective process. The potential of the payoff to society is enormous, but this must be demonstrated repeatedly and to the satisfaction of all.

We need to move quickly to adapt the techniques that will allow the automated storage and retrieval of information for the bibliographic control of the collection. Collection guidelines, if written in a form that allows for their automated storage and retrieval, form a picture of the entire collection which can be as general as the classification outline used or as specific as individual titles within it. This allows for two types of approaches to information retrieval: the user who knows the title or other specific bibliographic information can go straight to the catalog; the user who has only a vague idea of the best retrieval method can consult the collection guidelines and see a broad profile of the collection, finding perhaps the specific area sought or the variety of choices available. The individual titles can be located by consulting the shelflist or selected subject headings.

Information is the business of libraries; automation is the key to storage and retrieval of large amounts of information. Entering the collection development policy statement into the library's automated information system allows for retrieval of management data which can supply vital statistics regarding the library services and the use of the collection. When the library computer produces data regarding the numbers, types, and categories of items added, these figures can be correlated to the guidelines and to collection use from the automated circulation system. Selectors have the potential to see, in a very specific fashion, the results of their efforts. They can also use such tools to prepare for changes in the institution which require added or reduced library resources, and they can get a global perspective on the entire collection with one simple command.

Such evaluative techniques can only be used if the library's files are automated. Once this is achieved, however, bibliographic control of the collection becomes a part of the database which, if assembled thoughtfully, can yield extraordinary results. This database will contain information regarding the nature and use of the collection, as well as some general statements about the users themselves. In building various components into this database, it is important to keep in mind the necessity for flexibility alongside the goal of maximum automation of procedures.

Library administrators need access to the most accurate and timely information possible in order to justify the exorbitant expense of libraries to their funding agencies. Forecasting techniques and other evaluative methods will be in greater demand for the preparation of accurate and useful justification methods. For this purpose, it will be necessary to go beyond the collection policy statement to find out not only what the users want from the library but also what information needs exist for the nonusers and the reasons for lack of use. The leaders and change agents of the future will need to maintain a dynamic approach to the provision of information, which requires growth and reductions in the right amounts at the proper time. Collections will not be able to continue to grow like amoebas in whatever direction they will. Instead, the shape of the collection, in conformity with its stated goals, must be guided by selectors and other related personnel.

Libraries will find that, by articulating the breadth and scope of the collection, they will be making other decisions or redefinitions of the philosophy and goals of the library itself. It may be true that certain libraries in the future will seek to fill only the recreational needs of their users, while others will provide resources for educational purposes that support specific curricula. There will no doubt be a third category which will focus primarily on collecting and providing access to research-level material in specific subjects. Such libraries may be affiliated with universities or scientific organizations, or they may simply be funded by private corporations or professional groups.

It is important to form information networks in the future both within these categories and among them. This way, electronic access is available to many more institutions and users. The exchange of information and the sharing of resources can bring almost limitless power to the user.

Collection development strategies need to stay abreast of the changing needs of the environment of the library. In the academic or research world, collections must be adaptable to the varieties of formats in which information will appear in the future. While it is highly unlikely that, in our lifetimes, we will see the advent of the "paperless society," we are realistically confronted with information on every imaginable type of record in the coming decades. The diversity of formats can also provide needed options that will help resolve the serious information storage and preservation problems that large collections will face in the next 20 years. Libraries with collections oriented to a very specific and limited set of criteria may find that they can record the entire contents of their collection onto a handful of laser discs which can be kept in a safe place and referred to in the event something happens to the original material.

The dilemma inherent in the proliferation of information and the number of formats available is that finite resources, limited funding, and the impact of inflation prevent the ideal collection development from taking place. Educational institutions and publicly supported research libraries will quickly run out of space if they try to collect comprehensively in order to meet the current and anticipated needs of their users. They also cannot provide the ideal methods of storage and retrieval within the limits of their budgets. The definitions of academic and research libraries need to be reviewed, and the concept of comprehensiveness will need to be reexamined rather quickly. If material of an esoteric, research nature is only referred to infrequently by a small number of users, selectors should take the time to carefully evaluate its place in the collection. Resources in the nearby (or distant) geographic area will need to be more seriously considered as an alternative in the future. The notion of "owning" information will be greatly different from having access to it. Eventually, as electronic means of access become more common, it is certainly possible that researchers or other users will not need to travel to consult other resources. In fact, Gorman describes the "Electronic Library" as the answer to the "Paperful Society."[3] The cooperative endeavor he talks about involves the pooling of bibliographic resources in a region, making them accessible to all users by electronic means, thus achieving an integrated system from which all libraries, regardless of size, will benefit.

Collection development in the future will thus be integrally involved with resource sharing. Electronic means of access will resolve some fears that plague large libraries, such as the potential destruction of rare materials that, therefore, cannot be loaned or used outside the library. There may also be the side effect that censors will have a much more difficult time enforcing the current application of the law; there will eventually be complete access to the library's collection, as well as resources available through it, via a cathode-ray tube terminal located in the user's home or place of work. More sophisticated devices will have to be developed if enforceable limits of access are desired in the future.

Some of the more subtle implications of such resource sharing will require a redefinition of research-level collections, particularly in their attempt to be comprehensive. In some instances, absolute coverage of a subject or type of material is impossible, since some important materials are only available immediately upon publication, and in such limited numbers, that many collectors will miss them. Picking them up retrospectively could prove very difficult if they rarely appear in the antiquarian or used book market; few items in this category are likely to be reprinted. A library which does not have a long history of comprehensive collection efforts in a certain area will always be at a disadvantage without resource sharing. This means that, without it, a collection which must respond to the needs of its parent institution can be seriously hampered. Universities will not be likely to accept limits on the areas in which they can grow, even though limits may be imposed by the realistic collection activities which could take place in certain areas. In the future, one part of the selection decision will be concerned with the desired location of the item—that is, one copy necessary in the "home base" library in the city/state/region. Retrospective materials needed will have to fit stricter guidelines for collection efforts to be made, due to both the higher cost and the lower return on this category of acquisitions.

Electronic access to the resources of other libraries can change not only the nature of the collection but also the way in which the selection is made. All collection-related decisions will need to incorporate specific facts about the type of information required by the primary users, how the information will be used, and how often it will be sought, in addition to the availability and format of the information. Long-term goals of the institution and the collection also need to be considered in collection development as preparations are made for the changes coming the next century.

Selectors will have online access to the catalogs of other libraries; lists and catalogs of publishers will be available as another database by subscription; bibliographic information regarding current publications on the national level will be accessible as soon as it is entered into the MARC database.

Evaluation of material—whether book-in-hand or from a citation only—will take place at a cathode ray tube terminal, where the selector queries one or several catalogs before making the decision: if the title is rare or expensive, and of marginal interest, the selector asks whether or not it is already held at a sufficiently accessible library, in which case it need not be purchased. In another case, the catalog of a library with similar respon-sibilities and level of collection in a certain subject can be searched to see if it holds the output of a small, unfamiliar publisher. A third title is searched in the national catalog to see who owns it, what type of collection the library specializes in, and what similar titles may be held in common. In the case of another item, the holdings of the "home-base" library itself may be searched to find out what material is held on the same subject, what type of use it receives, and what category of user calls for it the most. For a different category of material, the figures on use of regional resources might indicate that it would be best to provide additional local access to items in that subject area. If this is true, the selector must be able to consult other indicators, including the collection guidelines, and be able to present a case to the policymakers if a change is indicated by the data.

Changes will be possible to identify and implement in a short time, and the selectors, or the interpreters of the collection, will be in the best position to propose or advocate them to the institution. This information about the collection use and the demands that are made from it will be only a part of the picture that leaders will need to see in order to guide collection development in the fashion most beneficial to the library and the institution. Important institutional requirements, such as the need to function optimally with a budget that has the same purchasing power as the previous year, are also part of this picture. As the demands of the institution change, and the purchasing power remains the same, or is even reduced by the total impact of inflation, the most significant contribution leaders can make is guidance of the collection into the most effective, beneficial areas possible.

Many institutions involved in education will find that declining enrollments will have a strong effect on their future. These administrators will be seeking ways to overcome the effects of such trends. One possibility will be the attempt to attract students from other categories of citizens, such as middle-aged and older people interested in ways to continue their education, to try for higher degrees, to advance in a field, or even prepare themselves for a different career. Trends in this country indicate that more women and minorities are already pursuing educations beyond high school.

Collections gathered for the recreational use of their patrons will have to deal with the same issues, from the diversity of formats in which the information is available to the need for up-to-date information about the use of the collection. Since the technology required to gain access to the various formats is just as important as the information itself, sometimes these libraries will need a system to allow patrons to rent or borrow it also. Perhaps alternate sources of funding will be sought in the effort to counteract diminishing sources of public funds.

Political involvement will be an important requirement of library leaders in the future, not only to keep in touch with the needs of the institution or clientele served but also to remain in a highly visible public position as representatives of an important and valuable social service.

Information brokers will be in demand in the future; librarians who are museum curators will have limited opportunities. Institutions which are responsive to the needs of their supporters will survive even inflation-eroded, limited budgets. Growth can only take place by pursuing productive activities; evaluation methods utilizing statistics produced by automated data processing systems can provide a workable method of analysis. For selectors, managers, or administrators, the product will also be the most effective tool of implementation. Information is power, and the versatility and flexibility of the information control system used by a library will become an asset to the entire institution. Librarianship in the future will be most heavily concentrated in providing information and in devising the best possible techniques for acquiring, storing, and providing access to it.

Looking back over the past 20 years, we can single out some important trends that have had a significant impact on our lives; to look forward and identify such trends is quite a bit more difficult. Issues regarding the impact of inflation or automation are certain to have a lasting effect on the quality of life in the future.

For librarians, a very important decision lies ahead: How will we manage in the future with the possibility of immediate electronic access to information?

Libraries could become known for their ability to provide information, or they could limit their mission to guardianship of the printed word. The difference between these two functions also implies the contrast between the success of the profession as brokers of a valuable service and its mere survival.

Libraries will have to become more specialized in their collecting habits in the future, some aiming to serve the recreational needs of the population and others taking on the educational and research-oriented goals. Materials in other collections will supplement locally held information so that no patron request will go unfulfilled.

Selectors in the future will have a decided advantage by having access to automated databases. A policy statement, also in machine-readable form, will describe the existing depth and breadth of the collection efforts, as well as future intentions. Selectors will have immediately at hand data about the circulation and general use of the collection, which will be combined with other studies for production of significant analyses of the library services.

Automated data storage and processing techniques will enable faster, easier access to information in the collection and provide accurate and timely statistics for planning purposes. In fact, without the recent advances in methods of data storage and memory capacity of computers, libraries would continue to be labor-intensive, inflexible, and costly organizations to maintain.

Resource-sharing networks in the future will make information accessible to users, regardless of their physical location; it may eventually be possible to examine information on a terminal in the user's own home or office.

Information, rather than books or microforms, will become the valuable commodity of the future. Leaders who are searching for innovative ways to resolve the problems accompanying inflation will focus first on collection development, since that constitutes such a large portion of the institutional investment. By taking the approach of collecting information, as opposed to buying books, much more flexibility can be gained. In the process, a more vital and dynamic definition of librarianship will result.

REFERENCES

1. Sheila T. Dowd, "The Formulation of a Collection Development Policy Statement," *Collection Development: A Treatise,* Vol. II, ed. Robert D. Stueart (Greenwich, CT: JAI Press, 1980), pp. 67–88.

2. Richard De Gennaro, "Libraries and Networks in Transition: Problems and Prospects for the 1980's," *Library Journal* 106 (1981): 1045–49.

3. Michael Gorman, "The Electronic Library, or Learning to Cope with the Paperful Society," *American Libraries* 12 (1981): 273–74.

Reference Service:
Software in the Hardware Age

by Carolyn Dusenbury

It seems, from empirical evidence and numerous reports, that we are in the midst of a "revolution." Since revolutions are better judged by hindsight, perhaps it would be wiser to say that we are in the midst of an insurrection characterized by the fascination about and the obsession with information and the delivery of it. Information, long relegated to the outpost of libraries, is now fashionable. More than fashionable, for, if the reports are correct, the next 20 years are going to do no less than rearrange our lives. We will engage in our occupations, transact business with the bank or the broker, and "go to" the movies without opening our front doors. For all we know, the door may open itself. Even fixtures like the daily newspaper will disappear, replaced by a databank which allows us to select information in a preprogrammed order and keep our hands clean in the process. There is a "gee-whiz" quality to all of this that seems closer to science fiction than real life. It is, however, confidently predicted that this is not an optional convenience; it is "the future"—you can run, but you can't hide.

Librarians are not alone in being at the same time anxious and dazzled by the prospect. Will libraries be transformed or be only cosmetically different from the way they are today? Some things are certainly going to change. Providers of reference service ponder a future in which the generation of information will continue at a fantastic pace, the modes of access will no longer be paper-based, and the expectations of our public may be very different. Planning and preparation are clearly in order.

Leadership is elusive in exact definition. If there is one encompassing idea, it is influence. The exercise of influence is that of making things happen, of mobilizing and organizing toward the accomplishment of goals. Leadership is the process of influence, of having the power and ability to assess, organize, and evaluate action toward accomplishment. It is, by any definition, proactive instead of reactive.

Reference service has been traditionally reactive, depending on creative survival and adaptation to change. Leadership is needed to anticipate coming events, formulate active strategies for service, and influence the decisions that are made.

How would this work begin? It must begin with a theory of reference service that will act as a foundation, allowing reference to anticipate, plan, and act.

What reference service *needs* is a theoretical formulation of what it really is, what it encompasses, what the nature of its content and substance is, and what its characteristics are. A theory provides a common ground for the resolution of issues, an organized way to apply principles to problems and practice. The existence of a widely understood and widely used theoretical framework is the best device to make things happen and to accomplish our goals of service now and in the future.

What reference *has* is practice, not theory. We study the traits of successful reference librarians and learn the value of intelligence, knowledge, humor, and good feet. We study the method of reference and learn search strategies and reference tools which are equally useful. We are imbued with the ethos of reference to go forth and be useful. We advance the state of the art by describing to others "how we do it good." We develop guidelines and standards based on assumptions, detailing how to put the assumptions into practice. If a thoughtful objection to any assumption is raised, we are at an impasse. These are not trivial concerns; they are the noise of practice surrounding a silent center. Why are these things as they are? What the underlying principles that explain and validate our practice? Without a theory of reference service, we will toil in ignorance.

THEORY OF REFERENCE SERVICE

The best way to illustrate the need for theory is to use it and see if it works. This will be attempted in the following discussion.

First, an abbreviated theoretical formulation will be developed. It is based on the work of Patrick Wilson in two publications, *Public Knowledge and Private Ignorance* and *Two Kinds of Power: An Essay on Bibliographical Control*. The disclaimer at the outset is that any abbreviation is, by definition, imperfect and incomplete. All flaws should be attributed to me and not to Professor Wilson.

After the theory is, however imperfectly, described, four of the many current and future issues in reference service will be examined to determine if theory can resolve issues and anticipate areas that will require resolution. The issues were chosen more or less randomly. They were not chosen because they were the most amenable to a theoretical solution.

Reference is usually characterized as the intervention of the librarian between the library user with an information need and the appropriate source to satisfy that need. These three parts do not perform in isolation but are viewed in combination as an interactive process:

Source◄─►Librarian◄─►User

or, as they are used in Wilson's description:

Public Knowledge ◄─► Librarian ◄─► Private Ignorance

PUBLIC KNOWLEDGE

Wilson defines public knowledge as ''the view of the world that is the best we can construct at a given time, judged by our own best procedures for criticism and evaluation of the published record.''[1] The definition is sufficiently versatile to include anything that is, or has been, known, whether it is part of the published record or not. This spreads the net of public knowledge very wide indeed and, because of the difficulty presented in any attempt to criticize or evaluate that which exists but is not published, this essay will limit the discussion to the body of knowledge that exists as the published record.

The size of public knowledge increases as the number of published records grows, but not every record adds to what is known. The task of interpretation or discovery of what is known requires

> more than a simple inspection. . . . It is a job of construction. . . . The task is not, or not, primarily, to increase our knowledge, but simply to say what it is. It is, then, not a job of original research, but it is a job of research: library research, or, as we shall call it, documentary research.[2]

Documentary research is a twofold enterprise, requiring internal criticism ''to determine whether what is said is consistent within the document,''[3] and external criticism which determines ''whether what is said is consistent with what other documents report, and to determine in general how it relates to other documents.''[4] The result of this determination may also add to public knowledge ''not by the conducting of independent inquiries . . . [but] by the drawing of conclusions not made in the literature received but supported by the part of it judged valid.''[5]

One of the manifestations of this process of criticism is the bibliographic structure of the corresponding body of literature. Literature will generate a bibliographic structure in some degree unique to itself. The bibliographic structure is also reflected in the reference works of a body of literature. The purpose of generating reference works is to condense a larger body of literature into a smaller body "containing only what is worth repeating"[6] in such a way that the larger body is accessible. Reference works are a section of, or a selection from, the body of public knowledge that constitutes "a deliberate survey of what is known in some area of inquiry, or a systematic presentation of all, or all of the most significant, facts in some array of facts."[7]

Wilson notes three types of organization for reference works: topical, disciplinary, and functional.[8] The bibliographical structure is reorganized in such a way that users in particular situations can more easily discover the appropriate part or parts of public knowledge. The criteria of relevance and future applicability[9] are used to prepare reference works for varying levels of sophistication and orientation to a subject by discipline, function, or topic.

The uses of reference works are also discussed in *Two Kinds of Power*. One's power over public knowledge is called "bibliographical control." Two possibilities exist. The desire of the first is the ability to find the best textual means to an end; the desire of the second is to identify all existing writings fitting a certain description. Wilson calls these, respectively, "exploitative control" and "descriptive control." They are not equal states:

> I suggest that, apart from the desire to be able to indulge one's whims and idle curiosity, the only reason for desiring that [descriptive] power is as a substitute for the other, greater, but less easily obtainable power. The only reason for wanting to line up a population in arbitrary ways is that one lacks the other power, and has oneself to attempt discovery of the best textual means to one's ends by scrutiny of members of various neutrally described classes of the population.[10]

The power over a collection of materials grows if one can make a variety of demands on the collection to increase the "range of control." Other dimensions of power are accessibility, response time, and reliability.

The greatest degree of exploitative control would result in "the best means to my and everyone else's ends, supplied instantaneously, effortlessly, and with absolute reliability, the supply consisting of the most suitable copy or performance in the bibliographical universe."[11] The greatest degree of descriptive control, under the same conditions, would supply items of any neutral description.

Wilson goes on to include the notion of relevance as central to bibliographical control. A distinction is made between "relevant" and "fitting a description," while these terms appear to be synonymous with the two kinds of power. Relevance adds "the measure of quality and utility of a body of writing available for use in problem solving."[12] Relevance is particularly important in the construction and identification of bibliographic instruments or reference works:

> To call anything that might be used, more or less successfully, for a bibliographical purpose a bibliographic instrument would be rather like calling everything a hammer that could be used, more or less successfully, to do one of the things that hammers are for . . . [13]

A bibliographic instrument is especially designed to list and/or describe other writings for a bibliographical purpose. This includes "detachable" lists that are intelligible when detached from the text of which they are a part. The specifications of such a list are that a work must be what it says it is; it must make plain the body of literature it encompasses; it must explain what parts of the literature were considered for inclusion; it must explain the rules under which it operates; and it must exhibit a system of organization to make the body of literature included easily discoverable. It is for this last purpose that subject headings, classification systems, indexes, and cross-references are necessary. Such systems to organize, index, and interrelate must be designed using a criterion of importance in order to create an auxiliary apparatus that makes the location of any part of the body easier rather than more difficult.

The upshot of all this is . . .

> to enable a thinker to get together what others have written on the subject, in order to build on that foundation, not necessarily just to avoid repeating work already done, but simply so that he will be in the best possible starting position, and will not be liable to repeat others' work unwittingly. [14]

Private Ignorance

Each person has areas of concern and areas of interest. "Concern is a readiness to act, to exert control or influence . . . [or] at least plan what to do if the catastrophe comes."[15] Areas of interest overlap areas of concern. "Interest in an area is simply wanting to know how things stand in that area, wanting to be informed."[16] Areas of interest are areas of idle curiosity, inquisitiveness, or any pursuit involving no commitment to action. The use of an information system is different in each area.

In pursuing either area, each person has three systems operating in an attempt to meet information needs.[17] The "monitor system" uses personal observation and communication in conjunction with the sources one uses routinely (e.g., magazines, television) in order to be informed at a desired level. The monitor system is at the same time purposive and incidental. The "reserve system" consists of sources which may never be used but which are available if the need arises. In areas of concern, a library is part of the reserve system. The "advisory system" is made up of those who are able to advise one regarding a specific decision. Advisors provide counsel in addition to information. Physicians, attorneys, and stock brokers function in the advisory system.

What one seeks to avoid in areas of concern is called "costly ignorance."[18] Ignorance which is harmless is of no concern. When we think we have enough information, act on the basis of that information, and suffer costly consequences as a result of it, then we are victims of costly ignorance.

Each person has a range of outcomes available in any decision. We do not seek the ultimately advantageous outcome but usually choose the easiest acceptable solution. We are motivated to mitigate costly ignorance dependent on the importance and need for a level of outcome as a result of our decision. Behavioral scientists have developed a substantial body of material on why this is so. Expectancy theory, developed by Victor Vroom, is the most straightforward and descriptive for the purposes of this discussion. The theory postulates that we are all motivated by a combination of three variables: the value of the outcome (valence), the effort to performance (expectancy), and the performance to outcome (instrumentality).[19] We establish the value or importance of an outcome combined with the effort it will take and the degree to which various levels of effort will lead to more favorable outcomes. If the decision is critical to our well-being, the model postulates that we will be motivated to expend greater effort in an attempt to achieve the most advantageous outcome. The importance of the outcome dictates how much information is enough to prevent an unacceptable level of costly ignorance. Often the process of gathering information is not enough; the process requires the kind of criticism described above. It is obvious that we prefer correct information to wrong information, but, many times, we cannot determine the "best" sources or cannot interpret them for our purpose. One cannot exert one's own exploitative control.

The Library

One of the places where public knowledge meets private ignorance is at the reference desk in the library. The discussion above indicates, however, that this is the exception, not the norm. Like other publicly funded institutions, libraries are part of the reserve system. "The need for a search for new sources . . . is a sign of failure of one's information system. Far from welcoming occasions for search, one wants no such occasions at all."[20] Wilson says this is analogous to the existence of hospitals or fire departments. The existence of such institutions, and their continued funding, is based on a hope that one will never need them but a desire to have them in case the need arises for ourselves or others. Any other view of libraries is seen by Wilson as sentimental and unrealistic.

The situation of libraries is complicated by the availability of the other systems. Libraries are not salient to most people who will choose easier avenues of information. They may rely on personal collections. If they need to know how to fix a faucet, they can purchase a single source from a bookstore to meet that need. This constitutes their definition of descriptive control. The idea of exploitative control, the absolute best way to fix the faucet, never occurs to them. They can always call a plumber, using the advisory system, and not deal with information at all. It is only when the information need cannot be met in these ways, or when one is unwilling or unable to use them, that the reserve system may be used.

Those who use libraries for areas of concern fall into three categories, according to Wilson. Each engages in a search as part of an occupational role.[21] They are the practicing professional, the professional researcher, and the student.

Because the body of public knowledge and the bibliographic apparatus are not the kinds of things that most users can subdue singlehandedly, the library provides the reference librarian. The baroque complexity of the apparatus and the selection of the appropriate parts for use makes interpretation necessary.

THEORY IN PRACTICE

The premise of this essay is that a theoretical foundation that is widely practiced and understood can help reference librarians resolve common problems and also help them anticipate the issues they will face in the next 20 years. A few of these current and future issues will be examined to determine whether or not the premise is correct.

Bibliographic Instruction

That librarians should offer formal programs specifically designed to increase the ability of the public to use libraries sounds reasonable and attractive, but it is no certainty. Many thoughtful statements have been made to the contrary [22] The skeptics feel that teaching is an inappropriate role for librarians, that instruction is a fad, and that the cost is too great for the benefit derived. Instruction is vulnerable to these arguments. Instruction librarians admit that no common technique or methodology exists. Frances Hopkins notes that, in most programs, instruction has ''been absorbed into the general consciousness as an adjunct to, more than a transformation of, conventional reference service."[23]

This assumption of commonality is, inelegantly stated, plain wrong. Instruction librarians, for the most part, have adapted the practice of reference to instruction programs, but reference and instruction are fundamentally different. Lacking a theory for the former, the latter has no theoretical foundation; the real problem is that, theoretically, reference and instruction are at such variance that the idea that one has its roots in the other cannot succeed.

The reference desk is the realm of the known question, the specific need. The concern of instruction is not with questions that are but with questions that might be, providing students with the ability to answer questions not yet posed. The known question requires the librarian to match a need with the appropriate bibliographical apparatus, the process of intervention in the definition of reference that began in the description of the theory. Intervention is impossible in the realm of the unknown question and, further, is what we seek to eliminate when we undertake the task of training students to conduct independent library research.

Instruction librarians have realized that instruction involves the ability to talk about sources, but the subject matter of instruction is not the provision of lists of sources with examples of the known questions they can answer. Instruction will only succeed when we provide students with an understanding of the nature of bibliography and its use. This sounds very much like the discussion of public knowledge. And, the content of instruction is precisely the mastery, at some level, of the bibliographical apparatus without the need for the intervention of a librarian. The student then should be taught how the literature of a discipline is developed, what its characteristics are, and how the bibliographic apparatus of that literature is a reflection of the literature. A student needs to know not only the content and use of specific sources but the place of those types of sources in the bibliography and the interrelationships among the various kinds of bibliographical instruments. This is the only way that a student can have any measure of power over the body of information and exercise any critical judgment over the sources. By teaching what an index, abstract, or encyclopedia is, and not merely what it does, we will help students conduct successful library research.

A complete description of how this can be accomplished is beyond the scope of this essay. The interested reader is referred to the works of Pamela Kobelski and Raymond G. McInnis for models of conceptually based programs that do what instruction programs should do.[24]

The controversy surrounding the need for any instruction is also, strictly speaking, beyond the limits of this essay. But, the opportunity to comment here is irresistible. If one accepts that education is, fundamentally, the progressive mastery of public knowledge, and that the purpose of education is to transmit why things are as they are, not merely enumerate what they are, it would be ironic (and more than a little depressing) to structure learning in such a way that the learner would not have, as a basic component of education, the ability to independently explore an area of concern or interest. Students at every level should be able to find information independently and should have been taught how to find the best information available. This is not an elitist idea designed to increase the status of librarians. That librarians should not do instruction is equally odd. The realm of the teacher is the content of the discipline; the bibliography of the discipline is the realm of the librarian. It is the content that is different, not that one group teaches and the other does not. Librarians are the logical candidates to teach the subject of bibliographical control. Instruction in the types of sources should be a progressive process at all educational levels.

Computer-Assisted Reference Service

The use of computers has become a routine exercise in reference service. With computer assistance, a librarian can identify the holdings of one's library, and of other libraries, and search databases more efficiently and in different ways than are possible in a manual search. The mass of information and the desire for currency in some disciplines have made computer assistance a necessity, a new part of the bibliographic apparatus reflecting the corresponding body of public knowledge.

A computer literature search certainly increases the descriptive control of the user. It produces items of a neutral description more rapidly, and it usually produces more of the body of literature than is possible in a manual search. The manipulation of the database by combination of sets with other sets yields a greater range of control with faster response time and reliability, three of the specifications of bibliographical control. For many users, the search not only provides items fitting a description but can also approach Wilson's notion of relevance. The searcher finds only those items that are very close to what is desired. One is provided with a high degree of descriptive control.

Exploitative control is, however, not possible in many databases. Those which can be manipulated by the use of citation analysis are the only ones that come close to providing the best textual means to an end. The identification of what McInnis calls the ''primordial source''[25] and the subsequent most critical citations (in the sense that they have been subjected to the greatest degree of external and internal criticism and also have been cited most often) yield a measure of exploitative control. This approaches Wilson's criterion of importance.

While the computer literature search improves the accessibility to all that exists in the universe included in the database, it is necessary to remember two things. First, the measure of control is limited to the degree that the database is an incomplete picture of the state of public knowledge in a discipline. Second, there is another measure of accessibility, that is, the ability to deliver all of the items discovered to the person who has discovered them. Wilson notes that ''universal physical access [in the first sense] is a librarian's ideal, but not an ideal with much attraction for anyone else.''[26] Identification is only half the problem; if the library does not own the material, the degree of power is diminished.

There has been much discussion recently of the issue of ''ownership'' versus ''accessibility.'' The present economic predictions argue against the former. Networks are the proposed solution to document delivery in the future. A pithy response to the advantages of accessibility rather than ownership is that of Michael Malinconico:

> One might argue that . . . the real value of a comprehensive national network is that it provides library patrons anywhere in the country access to materials regardless of where they are held. Such an objective is more pious than practical. First . . . the costly access mechanism provided by such a network will benefit only a very select elite, not the average library patron. Second, it is highly probable that all but the most sophisticated researcher would be equally satisfied with some alternative source obtainable with far less effort and cost locally. Third, it does not seem likely that someone in need of highly unique information would seek it in *any* library. . . . A national network of interconnected utilities will serve not the general library community, but a small highly exclusive elite. . . . For the majority of American libraries . . . a national network is quite simply a phantasmagoria . . . [27]

This seems to be an accurate appraisal, given the theoretical description of users of libraries. There are a few who will use the service, but, for the many, it constitutes an embarrassment of riches: not salient, not practical, or not worth the expense. Most library users desire to minimize the chance of costly ignorance with the minimum amount of effort.

The services of such a network for the serious researcher are uncertain. F. Wilfred Lancaster anticipates that, by the year 2000, some disciplines will have developed paperless systems.[28] He predicts that the scientific community will use a computer network, enabling those who generate and use scientific literature to collect data, explore the body of public knowledge, compose, critique, ''publish,'' and disseminate their work. Because the body of public knowledge is being expanded exponentially, and because the amount of what is known is also expanding, the theory predicts that the bibliography of the discipline will change as a reflection of that body of literature. Meeting the specifications of range of control, accessibility, response time, and reliability in such a system is not unimaginable.

If the network is too primitive for the few, and too remote for the many, one has to question its advantage to library users in light of the enormous cost and to question the emphasis by libraries on this solution to the exclusion of other remedies that would provide a bibliographic apparatus with the measures of quality and utility described by the theory.

COMPETING INFORMATION SYSTEMS

Information has become a commodity with a market value. The private sector has become increasingly involved in the information business. Commercially available databases are seen to be in direct competition with libraries. This would appear to be something of an overreaction for a number of reasons.

A commercial database will include only that which has a potential for profit, the heavily used rather than the esoteric. This is the kind of information that the monitor system provides for most people, which suggests that those who do not use libraries now may not use them in the future.

A commercial database with a necessity for profit may not meet the specification of reliability. Anita Schiller has noted that some of these services include advertisements and, therefore, have questionable reliability.[29] If the library can, as has been suggested, become a noncommercial but equally accessible information system that has the added feature of objectivity, it might be an attractive alternative. Library home-delivery systems might be comparable in cost and also provide library service to those who are unwilling or unable to come to the library. This would increase the salience of the library and perhaps many people would add it to the most used information system, the monitor system. If reserve systems are used when the other systems are judged inadequate, it is not expected that reserve systems will become obsolete. No database, alone or in combination, removes the need for a reserve system ''just in case.''

A commercial database provides only one kind of information. It can deal with a known item. One can get an answer to a specific question of fact. But, ''the use of known items does nothing to repair unknown faults in one's information system.''[30] To mitigate costly ignorance involves finding that which we have not identified. Wilson calls this a search for information.[31] Wilson divides reference assistance to users into three categories:

bibliographical assistance, question answering, and selection assistance.[32] A commercial database might take care of the question answering, but the other two would probably remain in the library as necessary functions in cases where one cannot exercise desired level of control or needs to evaluate more sources for more information.

The fundamental issue, then, might not be the existence of these services but the right to use the information. The problem is exemplified by "a growing set of restrictive arrangements now being asserted as the legitimate rights of one or another stakeholder."[33] The social imperative of right to use information must be preserved. While such restrictive arrangements raise a serious moral and ethical problem, in a more practical vein, the limitations on use drastically reduce one's power over information. The range of control, accessibility, and reliability are severely limited. The measure of quality and utility must be considered. The preservation of the right to have power over information and the protection of the intellectual process, rather than the existence of such systems, should be the foremost concern of librarians.

EVALUATION OF REFERENCE SERVICES

Meg Greenfield has asserted that "sooner or later, I have no doubt of it, we are all going to die of terminal social science."[34] Librarians are no longer trained in librarianship but in library science. To be "scientific" is all the rage. We build models to explain common sense; we use "paradigm" as well or as poorly as the next person. We have a collective mania to quantify. In many areas of the library, such data are useful and seem to be a political necessity. The attempt to evaluate and improve service and efficiency is not frivolous; but, as a tool to evaluate reference service, reference statistics are often useless.

The usual statistical method is to count the various types of questions (directional, ready reference, reference, extended reference) answered for those in the library and on the telephone during various times of the day. The body count can determine only the level of traffic. A large number of directional questions can mean many things. The sign system may not be adequate so the reference librarians may be directing patrons to the periodical room or the copy machine. Perhaps the librarians are taking every question at face value in the belief that what a patron asks for is what the patron really needs. The reference and extended reference categories may not indicate whether the question answered involved extensive bibliographical assistance or instruction or was, in fact, an extended reference question.

A better method has been suggested. It involves summarizing the reference question, search strategy, tools used, and the ultimate solution. The summaries are used to evaluate the performance of the libraries. This is the method most librarians used in their reference training, but reference is not practiced in an ideal time and place. No such system is complete unless one can weigh the situation—"paper due tomorrow," "four other patrons waiting at the desk," "patron could use only large print," "couldn't find five pages on the meaning of life." Unless such things are considered, we have examined the performance of the librarian in a vacuum isolated from the user. Reference, by definition, is an interactive process of the three components: source, librarian, and user. All three must be considered in the evaluation of the service.

From our description of the users of libraries, we can obtain very little useful information. We can ascertain how comfortable the user is and the relative satisfaction with the service. But relative to what? The best service and the best service for a particular need are not the same thing at all. The user desires to minimize costly ignorance, nothing more. The user is an unreliable source for scientific purposes. Relative satisfaction cannot be generalized or measured against an absolute standard. Each encounter is in some way unique.

This does not grant any smug immunity to reference librarians who can, and should, learn to improve their reference interviews, to improve their mastery of the bibliographic apparatus, and to have a better understanding of their clientele. But, the arbitrary application of social science methods is doomed.

Providing reference service is an art. The universe of unique questions and needs is infinite. The match of the need to public knowledge is not amenable to hypothesis or replication. The process is too unpredictable. There is no average library user and no average reference librarian. The approach to a question depends on too many intangibles. Any model predicting the time that should be expended on an average question of some type will result in poorer, rather than better, service.

The art of reference service was described by James I. Wyer in 1930:

> Reference work exists because it is not possible to organize books so mechanically, so perfectly, as to dispense with personal service in their use. . . . It still is, and always will be, imperative to provide human beings as intermediaries between the reader and the right book. . . . It includes and requires what may best be called *interpretation*, a far more delicate and difficult matter than can ever be achieved by mechanical marvels.[35]

That is probably the way it will be in the year 2000. It may not be elegant or efficient, but there you are!

CONCLUSION

This essay has attempted to illustrate the heuristic value and the real necessity for a theory of reference. It has been suggested that a widely understood idea of what reference is really about is the best device we have to look at what we do and where we are going. A theory can help us resolve the thorny issues—to know which questions have been answered so that we can move on to other controversial and interesting issues. Theory can help us to separate the real issues from the red herrings. Theory is central to all the peripheral racket. A theory of reference service does not need to be invented; it is there—to be taught to potential reference librarians and used by practitioners.

REFERENCES

1. Patrick Wilson, *Public Knowledge and Private Ignorance: Toward a Library and Information Policy* (Westport, CT: Greenwood Press, 1977), p. 5.

2. Wilson, *Public Knowledge*, p. 10.

3. Wilson, *Public Knowledge*, p. 10.

4. Wilson, *Public Knowledge*, p. 10.

5. Wilson, *Public Knowledge*, p. 11.

6. Wilson, *Public Knowledge*, p. 27.

7. Wilson, *Public Knowledge*, pp. 27–28.

8. Wilson, *Public Knowledge*, p. 31.

9. Wilson, *Public Knowledge*, p. 32.

10. Patrick Wilson, *Two Kinds of Power: An Essay on Bibliographical Control* (Berkeley, CA: University of California Press, 1968), pp. 25–26.

11. Wilson, *Two Kinds of Power*, p. 40.

12. Wilson, *Two Kinds of Power*, p. 50.

13. Wilson, *Two Kinds of Power*, p. 50.

14. Wilson, *Two Kinds of Power*, p. 135.

15. Wilson, *Public Knowledge*, p. 42.

16. Wilson, *Public Knowledge*, p. 43.

17. Wilson, *Public Knowledge*, pp. 37–38.

18. Wilson, *Public Knowledge*, pp. 61–68.

19. Expectancy theory is described in: V. H. Vroom, *Work and Motivation* (New York: Wiley, 1964); T. R. Mitchell, "Expectancy Models of Job Satisfaction, Occupational Preference and Effort: A Theoretical, Methodological and Empirical Appraisal," *Psychological Bulletin* 81 (1974): 1053–77; and V. H. Vroom, "An Outline of A Cognitive Model," and E. E. Lawler, "Expectancy Theory," both in R. M. Steers and L. W. Porter, eds., *Motivation and Work Behavior* (New York: McGraw-Hill, 1975).

20. Wilson, *Public Knowledge,* p. 84.

21. Wilson, *Public Knowledge,* p. 98.

22. See Jesse Shera, "The Role of the College Library—A Reappraisal," *The Role of the College Library—A Reappraisal in Library-Instructional Integration at the College Level, Report of the 40th Conference of Eastern College Libraries* (Chicago, IL: Association of College and Research Libraries, 1955); Anita R. Schiller, "Reference Service: Instruction or Information," *Library Quarterly* 35 (January 1965): 52–60; William A. Katz, *Introduction to Reference Work,* 3d ed. (New York: McGraw-Hill, 1978), pp. 260–65; Millicent D. Abell, "The Changing Role of the Academic Librarian: Drift and Mastery," *College and Research Libraries* 40 (March 1979): 154–64; and Pauline Wilson, "Librarians as Teachers: The Study of an Organizational Fiction," *Library Quarterly* 49 (April 1979): 146–62.

23. Frances L. Hopkins, "User Instruction in the College Library: Origins, Prospects, and A Practical Program," eds. William Miller and D. Stephen Rockwood, *College Librarianship* (Metuchen, NJ: Scarecrow Press, 1981), p. 173.

24. See Pamela Kobelski and Mary Reichel, "Conceptual Frameworks for Bibliographic Instruction," *Journal of Academic Librarianship* 7 (May 1981): 73–77, and Raymond G. McInnis, *New Perspectives for Reference Service in Academic Libraries* (Westport, CT: Greenwood Press, 1978).

25. McInnis, p. 93.

26. Wilson, *Public Knowledge,* p. 122.

27. S. Michael Malinconico, "The National Bibliographic Network: A Patrician Pursuit," *Library Journal* 105 (September 15, 1980): 1972.

28. F. Wilfred Lancaster, "Whither Libraries? or, Wither Libraries," *College and Research Libraries* 39 (September 1978): 345–57.

29. Anita Schiller, "Shifting Boundaries of Information," *Library Journal* 106 (April 1, 1981): 706.

30. Wilson, *Public Knowledge,* p. 85.

31. Wilson, *Public Knowledge*, p. 85.

32. Wilson, *Public Knowledge*, p. 100.

33. Schiller, p. 708.

34. Meg Greenfield, "Why We Don't Know Anything," *Newsweek* 92 (December 18, 1978): 112.

35. James I. Wyer, *Reference Work* (Chicago, IL: American Library Association, 1930), p. 5.

Leadership in Library Education

by Thomas J. Galvin

Given the assignment of addressing a topic as highly subjective and as ephemeral as "leadership," a highly personal perspective is probably inescapable. Recognizing this, let me state at the outset some fundamental assumptions or personal biases that must inevitably color the views I will express here on leadership in schools of librarianship for the next decade or two.

First, I write from the perspective of the chief academic officer (dean, director, chairperson) of a graduate professional school or department. With more than 20 years of viewing higher education from the point of view of an academic administrator, it is unlikely I could or would do otherwise. I do not suggest that leadership is exclusively the prerogative of the dean. Nor do I believe that there exists within schools of librarianship a neat division of labor under which the function of the dean is to lead and that of the faculty, students, and alumni to follow. It does seem to me, however, that, when a school or department of library science appears to lack a sense of organizational direction, it is the dean who must be held chiefly accountable for that lack. The office of dean, director, or chairperson carries with it both the opportunity and the obligation to play a decisive role in setting organizational goals and in establishing a clear collective sense of direction in moving the academic enterprise toward realization of those goals.

Second, the combination of experience and observation has long left me absolutely convinced of both the necessity and the inevitability of organizational change. Education for librarianship is no exception to the general principle that I have elsewhere termed Galvin's First Law of Institutional Dynamics.[1] In its most recent formulation, this basic principle reads, "Given a dynamic external environment, no organization can remain static. It is either expanding or it is contracting. It is either getting stronger or it is getting weaker. It is either getting better or it is getting worse." Assuming that continuous growth and change are both essential and desirable for library schools, two key aspects of the leadership role of the dean are, then, sensitivity to the optimal direction and pace of change and the capacity to manage academic change in a fashion that minimizes its negative effects on the quality and character of the educational program.

Third, I would postulate that the academic administrator is obliged both to recognize and to effectively come to terms with a set of environmental realities that can serve to severely constrain both the dimensions of leadership and the modes through which the leadership function can be exercised. For better or worse (perhaps a bit of both), the era of the library school as the lengthened shadow of its dean appears to be largely over. Few, if any, among us any longer command either the authority or the deference to set institutional goals or to mandate educational change by administrative fiat. Instead, we must embrace the strategies of collegiality and consensus building, while recognizing that even these more appealing leadership styles are subject to some fairly severe environmental limitations.

THE ENVIRONMENT OF HIGHER EDUCATION

The locus of education for librarianship will likely remain firmly fixed in the university environment for at least the rest of this century, so it is important to consider in some detail the major restrictions that setting imposes on the library school. These can be grouped into two broad categories—institutional resources and individual motivators.

The problems and perils of American universities in the 80s have been so widely reported as to require little elaboration here. Fewer prospective students, declining government subsidies (both direct and indirect), aging facilities, aging faculties, and steady-state budgets that reflect declining buying power with inflated dollars all combine to make finding the funds to finance educational innovation extraordinarily difficult. The consequence is that, at the very time when the need for change in higher education is most evident and most urgent, the fiscal environment seems least favorable to new educational initiatives. The additional costs inevitably associated with new academic programs cannot be met through incremental budgeting because, in most American universities, there is simply no unallocated money available. New activities can be funded, in general, only by re-allocating existing funds. If overall institutional funding is essentially steady-state, then a budget increase for one unit of the university means a decrease for one or several other units. Consequently, there is, and there is likely to continue to be, a climate of intense competition for funds among the several schools and programs within the university.

To one extent or another, academic budgets are at present most commonly enrollment-driven. Where fiscal leverage is a function of increased student credit hour productivity, library schools, which are typically experiencing level or declining enrollments, are hard put even to maintain existing budgets, let alone to compete for the additional dollars needed to support program expansion or improvement. Indeed, for some universities, the future fiscal outlook is so bleak that consideration must be given to closing down some schools and programs in order to release funds to shore up the remainder of the academic edifice. Smaller academic units with declining enrollments, which do not command either high prestige or large-scale alumni financial support, are extremely vulnerable in such an environment. Moreover, there is little tolerance for the kinds of financial risks that are commonly associated with educational innovation.

Similarly, the current fiscal environment offers little stimulus and few rewards for innovation either to the individual faculty member or to the faculty collectively. The range of available forms of tangible recognition for superior faculty performance has traditionally been limited in the academic world. Steady-state budgets, salary increments that are inadequate to keep pace with inflation, and the impact of collective bargaining all combine to have a marked leveling effect on faculty salaries. Faculty data compiled annually by Russell E. Bidlack for the ALA-accredited library education programs indicate that the size of library school faculties is decreasing, while both the average age of the faculty and the percentage of tenured faculty in library schools are increasing. Conversely, the number of new faculty being hired is decreasing, reflecting some loss of positions as a consequence of declining enrollments.[2] Given the collective impact of these several trends, the library school dean seeking to stimulate educational innovation is likely to encounter significant organizational and faculty inertia and an institutional environment inhospitable to both risk and change.

But, balanced against the severe environmental constraints that are characteristic of contemporary higher education are strong external forces that collectively constitute an imperative for fundamental modernization, revitalization, and reform in library education. Chief among these are the impact of new technology on the delivery of library and information services, the growth of continuing professional education, changing patterns of supply of and demand for new library and information professionals, and expansion of the private sector in the information field. Each of these represents a potential problem and a potential opportunity for traditional library education.

THE IMPACT OF NEW TECHNOLOGY

Media, microforms, computers, and telecommunications technologies have affected a radical change in the basic character of library collections, services, and operations in the last two decades. Their influence has been so pervasive that it is no exaggeration to characterize the professional education of those librarians trained up to 1965 as technologically obsolete. The implications for library schools are enormous.

Education for librarianship in the 80s and 90s must be heavily centered on the acquisition of a broad range of technological competencies and skills. Consequently, library education must incorporate a laboratory component similar to engineering education. This requires a large scale investment in the construction of instructional laboratories and in the acquisition of hardware, such as terminals, communications equipment, and media production facilities at a time when universities have little available free capital and few external sources to draw upon for capital development funds. Over and beyond these large front-end expenditures are the substantial operating costs of equipment maintenance and telecommunications which, to provide even a modicum of hands-on experience for students, would require doubling or trebling the current nonsalary budgets of some library schools. Yet, without a basic operational understanding of these technologies, library school graduates cannot function in today's libraries. Similarly, there is a massive need to upgrade the technological understanding and competencies of librarians now in service.

The problem is multidimensional. Not only must library schools somehow find the capital funds to acquire and maintain the needed instructional technology, they must also find a way to deal with the unfamiliar problem of meeting the high costs of rapid technological obsolescence, which requires frequent replacement of expensive equipment at intervals as short as five years. Perhaps most difficult of all, they must motivate and provide viable opportunities for senior faculty to achieve an understanding of these new technologies sufficient to incorporate their content effectively into established courses and curricula.

Accompanying these problems, however, are substantial concomitant opportunities to enhance the role of library schools. Between 1955 and 1975, library education grew rapidly in response to the urgent need to meet the demands of an expanding job market for new professionals. The schools were called upon to become largely "single-product industries," graduating greater and greater numbers of new MLS degree holders each year. The schools' other educational responsibilities, notably continuing education for professionals in service, were neglected or relegated to second place during this period. The present decline in demand for new entrants, accompanied by the growing demand on the part of practitioners for technological update, represents a fortunate coincidence of opportunity and need—a chance to reallocate faculty resources and to strike a new and healthier balance between preservice education and postgraduate, continuing education.

CONTINUING EDUCATION—RESPONDING TO THE NEED

Responding effectively to the needs of the community of practitioners for useful and accessible continuing education programs represents a major opportunity for academic leadership in schools of librarianship now and in the immediate future. Some of the more significant institutional obstacles that will have to be overcome in order to meet this need have already been enumerated. Human and institutional resources will have to be redeployed at a time when the university environment is not singularly receptive to internal reallocation. There are other potential barriers that must be recognized as well.

Continuing education differs in a number of significant respects from preservice education in librarianship. One major difference is that library schools do not, nor should they expect to, enjoy the same kind of educational monopoly. Unlike preservice education, where a degree from an ALA-accredited library education program has become almost the only viable route to full professional standing, library schools do not exercise exclusive control in the continuing education marketplace. National and state library organizations, networking agencies, individual libraries, state and federal government agencies, and private sector organizations have already staked out major territorial claims in the continuing education arena. Library schools are obliged to recognize these quite legitimate interests in continuing education. They are obliged as well to work collaboratively and in close concert with these other groups in joint development of an effective continuing education infrastructure.

The character of the need for continuing education is considerably more complex and varied than is true of preservice professional education. A relatively high degree of individualization in instruction is clearly required. Traditional content-oriented, instructor-centered methods of presentation are less well-suited to the learning requirements or the expectations of experienced practitioners. In some of the highest priority training areas, such as adaptation to new technology and development of effective management skills, the need to modify attitudes and behaviors (to penetrate what educators term the ''affective domain'') is as great or greater than the need to impart factual information or to develop skills. Finally, many of the traditional modes for the delivery of learning, such as the class that meets on 15 successive Tuesdays and Thursdays from 10:00 am to 11:00 am, are simply not appropriate or responsive to the audience to be served. In short, a major educational development effort is required to identify the continuing education needs of the library community; to devise, test, and implement effective ways of responding to those needs; and to create a viable infrastructure to support a national continuing education program. Substantial capital resources must be found to finance that effort.

If library schools are to play a leadership role in an emerging national continuing education program, then library educators must enhance their collective credibility vis-a-vis practitioners. In virtually every profession, it is commonplace for practitioners to characterize educators as being ''out of touch'' with the realities of practice. Librarianship is no exception to this view, and its widespread acceptance seriously compromises the credibility of library school faculty in a continuing education role. The simple fact is that library school faculty will, rightly or wrongly, be expected to demonstrate that they possess information, knowledge, and perspectives that are of value to practitioners.

It would be tempting to dismiss this problem as mere stereotyping if it were not recognized that some stereotypes are not wholly unrelated to truth. The fact is that accepting a full-time teaching position in a library school can rather quickly and easily result in a loss of effective contact with practice. In my observation, the library educator must first be able to recognize this as a potential problem and then work at finding ways to maintain a sound understanding of the reality of current library practice. The school and its administrators need to provide tangible support to the faculty in this effort. Sabbatical leaves, consultant opportunities, publication in those professional journals that are widely read by practitioners, involvement in the work of professional organizations, planning and conducting continuing education programs that are based on a systematic assessment of practitioners' needs and subject to rigorous consumer evaluation, and careful targeting of research projects in relation to high-priority operational problems are among the several avenues that need to be made widely available to library educators to assure that they can maintain continuous and effective contact with practitioners.

REVITALIZING THE CURRICULUM

The changing nature of the library job market has been widely recognized, and extensively discussed, by both practicing librarians and library educators. It is generally agreed that the profession is looking to library schools to produce fewer new graduates but, at the same time, to prepare individuals to function more productively and at a higher level than has been expected in the past. In response to what is perceived to be at once a quantitative and a qualitative change in the library marketplace, schools of librarianship are exploring and adopting a variety of strategies for curriculum improvement. These include strengthening instructional offerings in computer-based information technology, providing increased opportunity for specialization, and expanding internship and practicum programs in order to narrow the gap between classroom preparation and the reality of professional practice. To accommodate these and other curricular changes, a number of schools are giving serious consideration to extending the length of the first professional degree program, and a few schools have actually already done so.

Over the next several years, it seems inevitable that the concept of extended MLS programs will be vigorously debated among both library educators and practitioners. Even among educators, there is no evidence of even moderate consensus at this point. Some of the ALA-accredited programs clearly lack the faculty resources and instructional support facilities requisite to mounting an expanded program. Indeed, resources in a number of these schools, as Herbert White has rather forcefully pointed out, are seemingly marginal now in terms of even the present one-year MLS curriculum.[3] There is no clear ground swell of support among employers for extending the length of time required to earn, or increasing the cost of earning, the MLS degree. Grave doubts have been expressed as to whether libraries can or will raise beginning professional salaries to a level that would justify the time and cost of an extended first professional degree program.

Underlying all of these questions of curricular reform is the nagging suspicion that there are too many library schools and that the way to restore a favorable balance between the supply of new graduates and the demand to fill professional vacancies is simply to encourage or force some schools out of existence. Like most seemingly simple solutions to complex problems (and the supply-demand problem for the library profession is profoundly complex), the proposal merely to reduce the number of library schools is probably, in the words of H. L. Mencken, ''neat, plausible and wrong.'' In the first place, the supply-demand problem is as much a matter of distribution as it is of sheer numbers. The ratio between available jobs and available candidates varies markedly from region to region and varies within a given region between urban and rural communities. In the second place, the economics of library education, on both the supply side and the consumption side, provides little assurance that it is the higher quality schools that are also the most fiscally viable. Finally, there has been relatively little recognition or systematic consideration of the potential of schools, which up to now have defined their mission largely or exclusively as education for librarianship, to reformulate that mission in broader terms responsive to the rapidly expanding need to staff the emerging new information professions.

THE GROWTH OF THE INFORMATION PROFESSIONS

Perhaps the most striking phenomenon of the past decade has been the exponential growth of the information sector of the U.S. economy. By some estimates, information now represents more than half of the U.S. gross national product and more than half of the total labor force is employed in information-related activities. A more refined estimate, centering on the category of "information professionals," defined rather precisely in terms of job functions, was completed last year by the University of Pittsburgh and King Research Inc. under contract to the National Science Foundation. This study identified approximately 1,640,000 information professionals actually employed in industry, education, federal, state, and local government (but excluding health care) in the United States in 1980.[4] Some 10 percent of these individuals were employed as librarians, a total that correlates very closely with available census data. One may safely estimate that three-fourths of these 1,640,000 information-related jobs did not exist 20 years ago. It seems equally safe to predict that, if present industry growth trends continue, the number of information professionals needed will double by the end of the decade.

The demand for trained computer and information professionals—programmers, system designers, systems analysts, database managers, information services administrators—currently exceeds the supply of new graduates several times over. As the information field expands, it is also beginning to reflect a greater degree of job differentiation which can, in turn, be expected to result in more highly differentiated training programs. In particular, we can discern a growing distinction between training in computer science, which tends to focus rather intensively on the computer and its associated software, and information science, which views the computer as a mechanism in the information transfer process rather than as an end in itself. It is toward preparation for this broader professional role that some library school programs could potentially be reoriented.

The irony of the present situation is that, while many schools of library science lack both adequate numbers of prospective librarians as students and adequate numbers of library jobs in which to place their new graduates, there is an urgent need to expand training opportunities for information professionals to staff organizations other than libraries. The question, then, is whether existing schools of librarianship will make a conscious decision to explicitly broaden their educational mission to include preparing information professionals to function in nonlibrary environments and whether, having made that decision, they will be able to assemble the human and technological resources needed to support a redefined and expanded array of educational goals.

On the face of it, there are compelling pragmatic arguments in favor of enlarging the range of information-related fields for which library schools undertake to prepare their graduates. The fact is that, because of the constricted state of the current library job market, a growing number of new library school graduates are now obliged to seek employment outside the library field. Many have successfully done so.[5] Moreover, simply to prepare their students to function in contemporary libraries, schools face the need to make a major investment in technology and in the development of teaching laboratories. Such facilities can be designed so as to be readily adaptable to the support of courses oriented toward preparation for other information specializations. Given the necessity of such a capital investment, why should the schools deliberately restrict the application of that investment to a mere 10 percent of the jobs in the information field?

This is not to suggest that library schools should redefine their educational mission in terms of the *totality* of the information field. That would be an absurd and unrealistic goal. Programmers will best be trained in departments of computer science; electronic data processing specialists in schools of business administration; robotics experts in schools of engineering. But, there remains a substantial and growing field of professional employment, broader than can be encompassed under the terms ''library'' and ''librarian'' for which library education *is* eminently appropriate preparation. This is particularly true of those information positions concerned with data analysis and evaluation, information organization, information service management, and the design of information products and services in relation to the needs of information users.

THE GROWTH OF THE PRIVATE SECTOR

Closely related to the general growth of the information sector of the U.S. economy is the emergence of an expanding group of private sector organizations in the field of information products and services. These are typified by the membership roster of the Information Industry Association, a group that, up to now, has had only minimal contact with the library education community and toward which a large segment of the library profession has adopted a seemingly adversarial stance. Indeed, the expansion of the private sector in the information field is widely viewed as threatening to the established interests, clientele, and support base of libraries. Perhaps the most challenging issue facing the library and information communities in the decade ahead will be the redefinition of the economic basis of library and information services, especially with regard to the respective roles of the public and the private sectors.

Schools of librarianship are in a unique position both to facilitate the public sector-private sector dialog in the information organizations for trained professional staff. To do so will require, however, that library school administrators and faculty establish effective contact with information-related constituencies beyond the library community. It will also require a broadening of the philosophic base of the library school curriculum to accommodate such concepts as the marketing of information services, profit and loss, cost-benefit, and similar notions that go well beyond the traditional view of library service as a tax-supported "public good."

THE DECADE AHEAD

The next 10 years will inevitably offer a challenging group of problems to be addressed by those who assume leadership roles in education for librarianship. It will clearly be in the national interest to expand and strengthen the range of educational programs that serve the needs of the library and information fields. Some existing schools should unquestionably be phased out; others should be encouraged to narrow their missions to match available resources and the changing needs of the library marketplace; still others should expand significantly in response to the urgent societal need for trained personnel to design, create, and manage high-technology information systems and services. These major adjustments will have to be accomplished in institutions of higher education characterized by severely constrained resources and in a fiscal environment of limited development funds for which competition will continue to be intense.

To survive and flourish in such a period of rapid change and fundamental instability, schools of librarianship will require vigorous, confident, and creative leadership. If the challenges are great, the potential opportunities are even greater for library education.

REFERENCES

1. Thomas J. Galvin, "Beyond Survival: Library Management for the Future," *Library Journal* (September 15, 1976): pp. 1833–35.

2. Russell E. Bidlack, "Faculty," (Unpublished report, April 13, 1981).

3. Herbert S. White, "Critical Mass for Library Education," *American Libraries* 10 (September 1979): 468–81.

4. Anthony Debons, "Final Report on the Manpower Requirements for Scientific and Technical Communication: An Occupational Survey of Information Professionals," (National Science Foundation Project DSI-7727115, June 30, 1980).

5. Betty Carol Sellen, *What Else You Can Do with a Library Degree* (New York: Gaylord Professional Publications, 1980).

Leadership at the State Level

by Donald E. Riggs

State library leaders can anticipate exciting times for the remainder of this century. The return of federal funds and power to the states will require a more active leadership role from the state library agency and the state library association. This essay attempts to illustrate the dynamics of state-level leadership.

STATE LIBRARY AGENCIES

The future leaders of state library agencies will confront a more complex social system, a sharing of power, policy limitations, and even a controlling force imposed upon it by the expectations of others. State librarians are charged with providing responsible, creative leadership in an ever-changing society.

Essentially, the current functions of the state library agencies include:

1. The operation of special libraries and library services (law, history, legislative references, etc.) for specialized users.
2. Library development, especially support of public library development.
3. Supplementation of book and materials collections for local libraries.
4. Financial support to local and other libraries.
5. Facilitation of interlibrary cooperation through bibliographic and other finding and communication services.
6. Direct service to various unofficial users.
7. The maintenance of a large and comprehensive book collection.
8. The maintenance of an archives program.
9. The maintenance of a documents collection.
10. Promotion of library services in the public schools.
11. Services to disadvantaged users, including the blind, and to institutional populations.[1]

These functions differ among the 50 state library agencies. For example, several states are presently not responsible for library services in the public schools. Some states have initiated other functions, while a few states have taken measures in creating definitive subfunctions to the 11 traditional functions.

COPING WITH SOCIETAL CHANGES

By allowing one's imagination to wander a bit, it is not difficult to perceive the awesome responsibility placed upon the leaders of state library agencies as we undergo substantive societal changes throughout the 80s and 90s. The leaders will be required to make decisions based on a futuristic perspective of social transformations. New demands will be charged to state libraries for the provision of updated library services for the disadvantaged/handicapped, the urban dwellers, rural residents, and other special users.

The leadership role of the state library cannot be one of "wait and see." Rather, it must be one that keeps in step with progression on the social continuum. Wasserman notes this responsibility:

> The need for change in modern libraries is conditioned by many factors. It is conditioned by the changing physical characteristics of modern intellectual property, by the dictates of economy and efficiency in workflow systems of ever increasing scale. Most significantly it is conditioned by the human and the intellectual requirements of clientele. This is then more than simply a matter of procedure, of technique. It is a matter of purpose. For new social needs arise and intellectual requirements change. And the conventions and the programs of another age demand reassessment.[2]

The collapse of the provisional government in Russia during late 1917 was precipitated by the failure of the ruling leaders to change goals to meet a particular societal mood. Consequently, this leadership inertia placed Lenin in power. Societal values and beliefs will serve as the "lantern bearers" for the paths pursued by state library agencies. Adaptation strains will indeed be minimized if these agencies can learn adherence to and development of systemic balance in the values by society. If they do not, the inevitable will come about, as noted in Hamlet's prophetic warning:

> If it be now, 'tis not to come;
> If it be not to come, it will be now;
> If it be not now, yet it will come;
> The readiness is all.

LEADERSHIP FOLLOWERSHIP INTERACTION

Being a leader of a state library agency is, without qualification, one of the most difficult positions of leadership in librarianship. The umpteen constituents to be served, or answerable to, make the job nearly impossible. Each legislator, with pressures from "back home" constituents regarding what they want for their libraries, can further compound the leader's ability to be effective. There is nothing that implies that this crucial leadership position will be any easier in the year 2000.

It is incumbent upon those responsible for appointing the state librarian to conduct an aboveboard search and selection process whenever a vacancy in the position occurs. If the appointment is made in a sub rosa or unorthodox manner, the appointee may be ineffective with his/her followers from the very beginning and throughout a somewhat tumultuous, probably short-lived career. The position's legitimacy will depend on the followers' perceptions about how the leader obtained his/her position—the fundamental issue becomes whether or not the followers respect the leader and recognize his/her authority.

During the euphoria of effective program planning and implementation, it is mandatory for the leader to consult with library leaders from all types of libraries. If the state library agency prepares statewide goals with only "office" involvement, the goals will fall on deaf ears and receive little or no enthusiasm by the leaders in the field who will be affected by them. Participation by followers in goal setting and planning will enhance commitment and understanding throughout the state.

The consultation process between the state librarian's office and librarians in the field has undergone evolution during the past 20 years. Nonetheless, it is not hard to learn of state library agencies still operating in the autocratic fashion. It is my opinion that these agencies are in for a grand awakening. They will be forced to modernize their modus operandi (i.e., by a change in leadership) before they enter the 90s. I am not advocating a purely democratic-participative style of leadership but one that (1) discovers, via consultation, what library issues need attention, and (2) engages in open communication with librarians in the field while setting and striving for mutual goals. Diminution of esprit de corps should never be in the vocabulary of a state librarian.

The year 2000 will bring an appreciable improvement in the leadership-followership relationship. Few, if any, of the Machiavellians will exist at the helm of state library agencies. The successful leader will more than likely be technology-oriented, a humanist, the consult-before-act type, and someone who has charisma (not necessarily in this order).

TECHNOLOGY AND INTERLIBRARY COOPERATION

I am the master of my fate;
I am the captain of my soul.
Henley, Invictus

To quote Pulitzer Prize winner Robert Penn Warren, "Will man ride technology, or will technology ride man?" The librarian will continue to ride technology. There are only a limited number of procedures/processes in any library that can be automated. As a crude analogy, the computer is to today's library what the card catalog was to the library 100 years ago; that is, it is an instrument to use for achieving a particular task. Too many librarians have an alarmist attitude about automation; they think the machine is going to replace them. Most librarians do not understand computation, and computer people are equally ignorant about libraries. Nevertheless, and more importantly, the use of technology in any library or library agency in the twenty-first century will continue to be a positive, contributing force in the provision of improved services.

What will the state library's role in technology be by the year 2000? In addition to being the chief implementor of automation, it will serve the role of coordinator to ensure compatibility among the already established and yet to be installed computing systems. During the recent marketing of computing systems, several states installed systems which currently cannot "talk" with one another; there has been little leadership from state libraries in coordinating the installation of compatible systems. As a matter of fact, very few states have taken the initiative in developing interactive systems within their own states. Sometimes one gets the impression that various libraries in given states have intentionally purchased a circulation control system, for example, which is different from their neighbors' systems. This type of small-time competition and use of taxpayers' funds could be perceived as ill planning and, perhaps, is considered by some as a public scandal.

The state library must step forward with a statewide plan for automation, and it has to provide expertise in this area. If interlibrary cooperation and development are to occur in a modern, systematic mode, state libraries must utilize automation.

By the year 2000, nearly all states will have a complete bibliographic record of all catalog materials held by the various libraries in the state. This monumental and highly useful accomplishment will have occurred via retrospective entry of holdings in one of the major utilities (e.g., OCLC, RLG, WLN). One of the paramount goals of a state library, if it wants an effective interlibrary loan system, should be the attainment of bibliographic control of the state's library resources.

Document delivery, electronic mail, and laser transmission for information transfer will be common by the end of the 90s. The state library must be in the forefront of these new developments. Too many instances have occurred when the state library was the follower, not the leader, in promoting the use of technology.

ACCEPTING NEW BUDGETARY ROLES

The trend to switch funds from the federal to state governments, recently begun by President Reagan's administration, will continue. The keeping of larger percentages of the taxpayers' money in one's state is here to stay. The American public is interested in seeing less bureaucracy in Washington, DC; thus, the "dismantling" of various federal governmental agencies will continue. As a result of this movement, few, if any, library funds will be administered in Washington after 1985; they will be assigned to the state libraries for distribution, probably on a per capita/program basis. Consequently, the state library will need to take the lead in sustaining qualitative growth in federally funded services and programs. Administering the Library Services and Construction Act (LSCA) funds served as a precursor to budgetary experiences yet to come.

The complexities of state library agency operations will intensify due to the woes of financial setbacks and the unremitting pressures of inflation which will continue through the 80s. Naturally, the state library leader will have a difficult time getting more funds to keep existing programs afloat. State library budgets are already very small when compared with the budgets of other state agencies. I believe that the country's financial picture will improve dramatically during the 90s. However, struggling through the 80s with a stable/shrinking budget and a demand for more services will test the raw silver leadership qualities of the state librarians.

REDEFINING GOVERNMENTAL ROLES

The state librarian is often found between a rock and a hard place when trying to cope with all levels of government. A new sensitivity is required of state library leaders as they work with the many systems and networks which involve intergovernmental structures. Regionalization of libraries is evolving rapidly, but the question of who controls regional library activities (local, regional, or federal government) remains unanswered.

Joseph F. Shubert, state librarian for New York, describes, in the following, his concerns for leadership activities among the different levels of government:

> The natural tensions between local, state, and federal levels of government suggest another leadership dimension, and one in which we will see additional stresses over the next few years. In large part, the tensions are healthy, even as they are sometimes exploited as a means of buck-passing. Some of the tensions are related to perspective. Perspective is important in a state agency. Although no state librarian has a monopoly on it, the job helps provide that perspective (and often it is easier to work with a director, association president, or chairperson who has shared some statewide or varied experience). When tensions are strongest, definitions of leadership will vary. The same librarian who calls for "leadership without dictation" may be the first to call the state librarian and demand that he or she tell another librarian what to do. We hear demands for redefinition of local, state, and federal roles. By and large, the state library agencies have adapted and have been willing both to exercise initiative and yield responsibility as needs and situations change (as they did in early library "organization" moving from community to county to regional bases, training and continuing education, introduction of technologies). The way in which responsibilities are redefined and the process for achieving them may be one of the major leadership tests we face.[3]

STATE LIBRARY ASSOCIATIONS

Each of the 50 states has a library association. New Hampshire founded the first state library association in 1889. One year later, Iowa, Massachusetts, New Jersey, and New York developed their library associations. The last state to formulate its association was Alaska in 1960. New York has the largest membership with 4,000; California has the largest annual operating budget ($241,850). Total membership for all 50 states is 59,639; the total budget is $2,291,497.[4]

GENERAL ACTIVITIES

Events and activities generally found in a state library association's scope include (1) planning the annual conference, (2) reviewing and updating the constitution and by-laws, (3) addressing intellectual freedom issues, (4) conducting divisional/sectional/round-table meetings, (5) producing a journal or newsletter, and (6) generating social events. All of these activities are important; they provide the only formal gathering and continuing education opportunity for many library employees, particularly the clerical staff. The camaraderie furnished by the association's activities serves as an excellent therapeutic function in the lives of these library employees. Laypersons, trustees, and library employees from all types of libraries hold membership in these organizations.

LEADERSHIP INFUSION

Based upon my experience with four state library associations (having served as president of the Colorado Library Association and the West Virginia Library Association), I have observed that an enormous amount of time is spent on routine, but necessary, association matters. My message to the associations was to place more emphasis on long-range goal setting, creative leadership, and risk-taking endeavors.

The broad-intent, overall goal for nearly all associations is that of advancing/promoting libraries and librarianship in the state. This is a formidable pursuit; however, the "how is it to be done" ingredient is not usually reflected in the association's communiqué, nor is it firmly established in the minds of its members. A plan of attack on recurring problems and challenges needs to be set forth. This blueprint must include a time-phased, programmatic component in order to ensure continuity during the change in officers, which normally occurs every year and which is detrimental to getting high-priority, time-consuming projects completed.

The length of term for the president and executive board should be at least three years. One-year terms serve only, at best, as an introductory period to the problems and challenges. Serving as president of a state library association for one year is a prime example of trying to lead through limits. How much can one expect from his/her leader in one year? During this brief stint, the leader of the association has to infuse vision, energy, and drive into the organization, in lieu of practicing blandness and safety. A sense of continuity has to be maintained in the organization by each of its one-term leaders; nevertheless, the leader must be able to clarify problems by elevating them into understandable choices for the membership and to separate the important from the unimportant.

With the shift of emphasis for many of the social and educational programs from the federal level to state level, the state library association may be in a greater pivotal position than ever before. Regardless of what happens as this shift in power unfolds, it is not uncommon today to find, in some states, that approximately 90 percent of all funding comes from the local and state level. If LSCA funds are eliminated, some libraries may proudly acclaim that all of their funding sources are within the state. What does all this mean for the future? Simply put, it means that library leaders will expend more energy at the state level, rather than gallivanting about the country with little repayment (in the way of funds) realized. Furthermore, one can surmise, if the foregoing becomes reality, that leaders who are responsible for moving their libraries forward (financially speaking) may be forced to be more active at the state level.

The leader of a state library association will only be as effective as the membership permits. Petty jealousies and counterproductive activities are expected, but they must be minimized. Achievement of common goals, however, must remain uppermost in the intentions of the membership, if the necessary progress is to be garnered.

Leadership functions in organizations like the state library association will continue to be constrained by the attainment of task success which is tied to group maintenance. The leader must do what is required to maintain the membership by encouraging and sustaining a feeling of cohesiveness.[5]

Leadership in the state library associations by the year 2000 will be different in the following ways: (1) the very best leaders in the state will be encouraged and self-inspired to compete for the presidency of this proactive group, rather than having their current lackadaisical attitude; (2) the term of office in some states will be increased beyond the one-year limit: (3) well-developed, fully delineated organizational goals will be commonplace; and (4) the leadership position will be one of chief prominence within the state, and leaders from the 50 states will meet regularly to seriously compare notes and to discuss collective and unique strategies for greater successes.

THE LEADERS' SYMBIOTIC RELATIONSHIP

To be effective, leadership of the state library agency and the state library association must be congruent. A hand-in-glove, rather than a competitive, relationship has to exist. Too many times, library legislative programs have been lost due to lack of cooperation. When state funds are in short supply, legislators are amused by testimony from the state library association which is contrary to and cancels out justification given by the state library agency, or vice versa.

Working in harmony should not be perceived as dampening the creative processes by either group. If one leader prefers to operate with a "roll-your-own" style, the other one should be at least fully apprised of what end products are desired. However, creative strategies involving the legislators have to be planned in unison; both parties must be "singing the same song" while working with the lawmakers. The lobbyist, if employed by the association, should know where his/her orders are coming from and should be encouraged to work harmoniously with the state librarian.

Development of mutually agreed-upon goals for library improvement is perhaps one of the most fruitful endeavors to be undertaken by the two state groups. An example of this goal setting experience occurred in Scottsdale, Arizona, during the spring of 1981. The Arizona State Library Association called a meeting of library directors (including the state librarian) to discuss priorities and goals for the state. After this and subsequent meetings, mutual priorities were identified. During the entire experience, the state library was considered central to all discussions, particularly in how the priorities were to be achieved.

Never should the state library association be the "whipping boy" of the state library agency; neither should the state library agency be a "pawn" of the association! Both must be active leaders; neither should be submissive in any way to the other. Shubert gives his perspective on the relationship:

> The concept of unique and often complementary roles of the nongovernmental organization and the government agency in the United States is difficult for many overseas librarians to understand—and its practical applications occasionally may confuse some people at home. Within our 50 states there are considerable differences among the states, ranging from some in which the activities and voices of the state library agency and the state library association are almost indistinguishable, through what I would term healthy relationships, to those in which appears to be an almost complete standoff. Building a mature working relationship and a healthy respect for differing roles and responsibilities requires leadership skills on the part of both the state librarians and other professional leaders in the association. Increasingly, the same principles will apply to relationships with regional networks, which may operate on a multi-state basis but which inevitably must recognize the federal nature of our system. I think the healthy relationship develops best out of a problem-solving, consultative approach which recognizes and respects the fact that differing roles require different postures. The position of a state government's chief library officer can be both confining and advantageous, producing both opportunities and problems in working with a state association that often (but not always) has parallel interests. The leadership tests of the state librarian in this situation may be: Are things happening? How is credit shared? Who is listening? Are ideas surfacing?[6]

REFERENCES

1. Phillip Monypenny, *Library Functions of the States* (Chicago, IL: American Library Association, 1966), p. 6.

2. Paul Wasserman, *The New Librarianship: A Challenge for Change* (New York: Bowker, 1972), p. 11.

3. Letter from Joseph F. Shubert, State Librarian and Assistant Commissioner for Libraries, The State Education Department, Albany, NY, October 29, 1981.

4. *The ALA Yearbook* (Chicago, IL: American Library Association, 1981), pp. 325–77.

5. Edwin P. Hollander, *Leadership Dynamics* (New York: The Free Press, 1978), p. 89.

6. Letter from Joseph F. Shubert, October 29, 1981.

The American Library Association: Its Potential Leadership Role

by Elizabeth W. Stone

THE IMPACT OF LEADERS

> We meet to provide for the diffusion of a knowledge of good books, and for enlarging the means of public access to them. Our wishes are for the public, not for ourselves.[1]

The year was 1853; the occasion was the Librarians' Conference in New York City, attended by 82 delegates; the speaker was Charles Coffin Jewett, delivering the first presidential address at a library convention.

> For the purpose of promoting the library interests of the country, and of increasing reciprocity of intelligence and good-will among librarians and all interested in library economy and bibliographical studies, the undersigned form themselves into a body to be known as the American Library Association.[2]

The year was 1876; the occasion was the organizational meeting of the American Library Association, attended by 103 delegates (90 men, 13 women); the maker of the motion that was adopted was Melvil Dewey, who was elected secretary and treasurer of the newly formed association. Later, Justin Winsor, who was elected the first president of the Association and who served from 1876 to 1885, commented on that opening meeting: "We came together largely pervaded with the idea that a library was in essential a missionary influence, that the power which belonged to it needed consolidating and directing. . . ."[3]

Jewett, Dewey, and Winsor were all acknowledged leaders in the profession. They were perceived by their contemporaries to be out ahead, beckoning others to follow them. They enlarged, in the minds of their contemporaries, the possibilities of what they could do. In studying the early speeches and articles in *Library Journal*, one has the sense that people came away from the meetings they led with a sense of new places to go, new ways to get there, new ways to deal with problems, or new definitions of problems. As members of a profession, in a classification posed by Cyril Houle,[4] they were "innovators" attracted to new ideas and practices that seemed to offer high promise of success, even if not yet tested. Creating libraries and serving the public were goals which the profession, under such leadership, considered its urgent business.

Forty-eight years later, William S. Learned commented that the Association was "doubtless the most single important single factor in public library development that has come into being," although the founders of ALA consisted largely of librarians in private libraries. It was, he continued, "the beginning of a true library profession, and since its founding, it has contributed immeasurably to the building up of a substantial library science and to the education of the American public in the use of books."[5]

During these early years, ALA was viewed as being, and indeed was, in a leadership position with respect to the public library movement. Today, its stated goal is much the same as it was in 1876:

> The American Library Association is an organization for librarians and libraries with the overarching objective of promoting and improving library service and librarianship.[6]

It is understood that the "promoting and improving" includes all types of librarians, libraries, and library services. But, there is another difference—a difference in the perception of the organization, for today it is seen by many in a "following" capacity. ALA is perceived as not being on the real frontier, but in what historians call the "settlement," where territorial gains are consolidated. In other words, it is viewed as an endorser responding to and seconding the activities of other groups who are venturing forth or are seen as doing so. It is laudable to be an endorser or an approver, to borrow the best from other disciplines, and to consolidate gains, but it is not the same as being a leader, originator, innovator, or even a pacesetter.

The impression of some is that ALA has been so busy encouraging applications of new knowledge and techniques that it has failed to see and lead the development of the *next* breakthrough for improved library service as rapidly as the situation demands. Thus, if one applied Houle's classification of professional persons to the Association as a whole, it would probably fall not with the "innovators" or the "pacesetters," but rather with the "middle majority," where innovations are gradually accepted by people who "eventually adopt new practices because they have become so generally accepted that colleagues and clients would raise questions if older techniques were used." These people, Houle continues, may pay lip service to the idea of continuing education, "but it is hard to win their attention to a specific learning activity and harder still to persuade them to participate in it.''[7]

Some have suggested that one reason we spend so much time at ALA meetings endorsing and approving is that we do not feel comfortable with, or even know, what our mission is. (Beyond a general mission statement, we need to understand our statements of special goals and objectives.) This vagueness results in a tendency to adopt the central concerns of other groups and, sometimes, to speak disparagingly of some of our *own* central concerns. For example, how to facilitate access to information is a concern we should be proud of, and one we should be trying constantly to improve, with our heads held high, not just in the settlement but on the frontier.

SENSITIVITY TO CHANGE

In leading into a discussion of some of the areas in which I believe ALA could, should, and will play a leadership role in the coming decades, I want to focus some remarks on the need of all the membership to understand, accept, and deal with the reality that many fundamental changes will come about in the world surrounding the institutions in which we work. According to Malcolm Knowles, ''the most visible and universal characteristic in all professions in the next century will be change.''[8] This reality must become clear in the thinking of all of us in the Association if we are to achieve a working consensus to consider who we are, where we are, and where we are heading as an Association.

Circumstances affecting the development of library services will be different from those we have known in recent years. Without presuming to forecast in any precise sense what is going to happen, we can and should begin thinking about important changes that may stand before us, so that all of us who are concerned about ALA's role in the profession can plan accordingly. The Association has the capacity to lead, to stay ahead, and, given the vast changes that surround our activities, we must think carefully about how we are to continue to meet the needs of those we serve.

These are not simple times; indeed, they are times of monumental complexity. The world has become interdependent to a degree that would have been thought impossible a few years ago. Anxiety about future change tends to sap the self-confidence of leaders and to create in them indecision as to what the "right" decisions are. This emphasizes the seriousness of the risks we must take. It seems clear that the next two decades will be more difficult to cope with than were the last two, difficult as they may have seemed at the time.

LEADERSHIP HYPOTHESES

In a recent study of some 80 top administrators of academic institutions,[9] four "umbrella" characteristics of effective leadership were identified from a long list of hypotheses. The consensus of those interviewed was that a leader must (1) provide a sense of direction, (2) project a sense of enthusiasm, (3) furnish a structure for implementation, and (4) be willing to make decisions. These are skills that Jewett, Winsor, and Dewey also possessed. In the past, it was possible for one or two leaders to provide the dynamic qualities that would move an organization forward in a leadership capacity. But, in the future, in a society rampant with catastrophic changes, an organization with some 37,000 members will require not just strong individual leaders but the combined leadership skills of a committed executive board who, as a group, will exhibit those "umbrella" characteristics.

In addition, as Michael Maccoby, director of the Harvard Project on Technology, Public Policy, and Human Development, states in his most recent writings: "The ideal leader brings out the best in a group or country or society. He inspires cooperation, making for a team of winners rather than a group of workers of whom only a few will rise to the top."[10] Maccoby believes that the most effective leaders today exhibit the elements of flexibility, self-development, and participation—in other words, willingness to share power with those they lead.

In summary, the executive board of ALA must be concerned about the development of leadership skills, the continued renewal of the desire and the capacity to lead, the search for strengths and weaknesses, the generation of cooperation and participation among as many of the association members as possible, and the charting of personal development in the belief that how well they perform does make, and will make, a difference to the future of the Association.

STRATEGIC PLANNING

Looking to the future, ALA cannot and, I believe, will not be satisfied to live in a state of complacency; rather, it will find and develop leaders who will ensure ALA's leadership role with respect to library activities in the U.S. and who will help make ALA a leader among professional organizations in this information age.

There is, at the present time, no formal mechanism within ALA which gives, to one office, the authority and responsibility for overall planning. In order for the Association to assume a leadership role, I foresee that the executive board of the Association will assume responsibility for giving direction to the national organization. Such action would be in keeping with the sense of the final report of the Special Committee to Review Program Assessment Process and Procedures published in 1981. The report notes that:

> In order for the Association to continue to function as the spokesperson for all library interests in the United States, stronger leadership on the part of its managerial board (Executive Board) is essential. . . . We are unanimous in focusing on the Executive Board's responsibility to assume a leadership role in coordinating and giving direction to the planning, budgeting, and evaluation processes for the Association as a whole.[11]

To meet the leadership role of the Association, the executive board will engage in continuing strategic planning. This activity will provide a "critical road map for the organization to cope with future threats and to capitalize on future opportunities consistent with the Association's basic mission."[12] It will enable planning, budgeting, and evaluation to take place together.

Strategic planning calls for the continuing identification of external trends which could have an impact on the Association, such as inflation, the rapid development of new technologies, changing values held by individuals as to how they should use their off-the-job hours, and the predicted emergence of "the electronic cottage" as a new center for the production of goods and services (as envisioned by Alvin Toffler in *The Third Wave*).[13]

Strategic planning also calls for identification of opportunities, such as the recognition of the importance of information in society as a whole, the desire for participation on the part of individual members of the Association, the need for continuing education to achieve career success, and the lowering of the costs of new technologies which will aid in the development of new delivery systems.

Strategic planning also calls for careful attention to the three aspects of the Association's internal situation: its vulnerabilities or weaknesses, its strengths, and its key leverages. The Association's vulnerabilities cry for greater attention to the identification of, and response to, the needs of individual members, thus providing powerful motivation for joining the Association; programming that images forth an integrated whole rather than a multitude of parts; the need, as Houle has pointed out in speaking of ALA, for the Association to "strike an appropriate balance in the attention given to the special interests of the membership"[14]; and the need to strengthen the Association's relationships to its chapters and to improve communication with its chapters. Also, there is the need to solve the confusion and conflict over who, how, and when member services should be delivered. Additional emphasis needs to be given to better financial data and internal management of financial resources.

Strategic planning also calls for identification of the strengths of the Association, such as its publication program, including excellent reviewing services of many types of literature; new and impressive physical facilities at headquarters; an effective Washington office concerned with promoting the profession's interests in legislation; strong professionally oriented personnel at headquarters; and dedicated persons who are eager and willing to give volunteer service for the organization.

Out of the analysis of strengths and weaknesses will come the development of primary leverages which the Association can use to strengthen its leadership of the profession. These may include activities such as:

1. The expansion of the publishing program to include wider production of cassettes, videodiscs, and computer-assisted learning programs in identified areas of high demand.
2. The development of a comprehensive continuing education center.
3. Increased consulting and specialized services to chapters at the grass roots levels.
4. Planning for the growth of chapters.
5. Periodic workshops for the development of ALA leaders at the national, division, or chapter level.
6. Expansion of the headquarters library to serve as an information center for the membership as a whole, especially for those in positions of leadership.
7. An increase in the international activities of the Association, especially in the area of dissemination of its publications.
8. The furtherance of trans-border data flow.
9. Greater interactive planning with other associations with similar interests.
10. The adoption of a leadership role in sponsoring research.

For each key leverage identified, objectives, key strategies, action plans, and programs will need to be developed, with specific time frames established. These will need to be reviewed each year and new strategies developed to meet changing conditions so that the effort becomes not a "strategic plan" but "strategic *planning*." Primary responsibility for this effort will rest with the executive board and its committees (in close cooperation with the executive director), as it is the body identified by the ALA Constitution as responsible for leadership and management of the Association.

The importance of strategic planning is highlighted in the following statement based on experience of the American Marketing Association:

> While we may not be able to accurately predict the future, it is imperative that a voluntary organization develop a strategic plan for the future. Not to do so suggests that there will be no future.[15]

LIFELONG LEARNING

In the words of Malcolm Knowles:

> The greatest threat to civilization in the next century is not going to be war or pollution or disease. It's going to be the impending obsolescence of man, and particularly in the professional segments of society.[16]

In his latest book, *Continuing Learning in the Professions,* Houle challenges the professions to broaden their view of the concerns of continuing education beyond mastery of new knowledge and skills and keeping up to date with new developments to encompass the 14 goals which he identifies as the characteristics of an occupation in the process of "professionalization." This last term he applies to all occupational groups (including the oldest of the professions) which are striving toward the improvement of certain identifiable aspects of their occupation. Thus, not absolute criteria (termed "canons"), but rather dynamic criteria (termed "characteristics"), should be applied to professions. To clarify this concept, Houle gives this example:

> A canon might be, "A profession must have a clearly formulated code of ethics." A characteristic might be, "a professionalizing occupation should be concerned with the continuing refinement of ethical standards that characterize its work."[17]

Thus, a Houlean "characteristic" is a process, as opposed to a norm, and these characteristics take the form of goal-reaching behaviors on the part of a professionalizing occupation—behavior which is constantly changing because of the relationship of that occupation to society. Houle goes on to list the 14 characteristics by which he identifies an occupation in the process of professionalization. This process, he reminds us, may be carried out on many fronts at the same time. In other words, professionalization is never an improvement fully accomplished but is, rather, a pilgrimage toward improvement.

Houle's thesis is that a responsible profession should seek ways to exhibit all of the 14 characteristics identified with professionalization and that, in the broadest sense, continuing education is concerned with each of these. Summarized here are 14 characteristics which he identifies as performance or collective identity characteristics[18]:

1. Clarification of the profession's functions in society, by involvement of as many members as possible and recognition of the nature of its evolving mission. Once accepted, the new concepts contained in the mission need to be practiced.

Performance Characteristics

2. Mastery of theoretical knowledge.
3. Capacity to solve problems.
4. Use of practical knowledge.
5. Self-enhancement (including the development of new dimensions of one's personality).

Collective Identity Characteristics

6. Formal training.
7. Credentialing.
8. Creation of a subculture.
9. Legal reinforcement.
10. Public acceptance.
11. Ethical practice.
12. Penalties.
13. Relations to other vocations.
14. Relations to users of services.

By the year 2000, it can be predicted that ALA will have a Continuing Education Center—a centralized coordinating unit for continuing education activities at headquarters. One of its goals should be the maintenance of a nationwide "university without walls" for continuing information science and library education. It should offer an array of resources and activities which would offer support in all the 14 characteristics of a responsibly coherent profession suggested in the preceding paragraphs.

Another goal of the Center would be that of supplying all members with an equal opportunity for continuing education so that they may be lifelong students, regardless of geographical location. Local inadequacies will need to be minimized or eliminated by the use of new technology. Available knowledge and tools will need to be drawn from the fields of library and information science, the behavioral sciences, communication theory and technology, and other related disciplines and integrated into efficient means of educational production.

Opportunities will, in this conceptualization, be continuously provided at times, places, and paces convenient to practitioners. For example, individual learning opportunities at home or in the library will be reinforced by interrelated self-instruction modules and group learning opportunities will be available in libraries, which will, thus, be continuing education centers both for those in the profession and for those in the communities served.

The Center would, as I see it, have as a guiding principle that the opportunity for continuing education should be available at times, places, and paces convenient for individual practitioner-learners. Thus, the Center would recognize and focus on individual learning requirements, including individual participation, personal satisfaction, freedom of choice, continuity, accessibility, and convenience.

The Center would want to use technical means, such as the videodisc, to give practitioners opportunities to learn in an orderly, sequential way, at their own places, times, and paces. Such recorded instruction would need to be available in libraries and would permit repetition for broadcast by satellite and and cable or would be easily accessible to individuals wishing to study on their own. Materials should be available at various levels of complexity.

Evaluation methods must be incorporated into the materials that are developed. Practitioners may elect to take examinations or not, either anonymously for self-appraisal purposes or in order to receive credit. In addition, self-assessment tools could be developed which would permit individuals to discover how well they meet performance standards that have been developed for particular tasks through research performed or sponsored by the Center.

Beyond offering resources and materials, the Center would develop a network of continuing education consultants throughout the nation who, with the support of the Center, would help individual members develop appropriate self-directed learning activities which would enable them to perform their chosen roles within the profession with competence or to develop new knowledge and skills to match new roles.

The Center would consider certain basic concepts as working policies for its activities. These following seven concepts are presented by Houle as a program for action suitable for a concerned profession[19]:

1. The primary responsibility for learning should rest on the individual.
2. The goals of professional education, including those of continuing learning, should be concerned with the entire process of professionalization.
3. Continuing education should be considered as part of an entire process of learning that continues throughout the life span.
4. The patterns and methods of continuing education should be planned and conducted in terms of one or more of three modes of education: inquiry, instruction, and performance.
5. The provision of continuing education should expand so that it pervades all aspects of professional life.
6. Professions should collaborate on the planning and provision of continuing education.

7. The processes of recredentialing should be thoroughly rethought and redeveloped to determine the appropriate role of continuing education.

The pursuit of an action program embracing these components would constitute a challenge to set forth a pilgrimage in which the ALA, its individual members, its divisions, its state chapters, its round tables, and its other units could, in collaboration with other professional associations, help and support one another.

The encompassing overall goal of the Center would be to help ALA as an organization to be a "learning community" which encourages, supports, and provides resources for the growth of all.

PROMOTION AND USE OF THE NEW TECHNOLOGIES

Toffler provides a perspective on the new technology in the following:

The new electronic mode of production makes possible a return to cottage industry on a new, higher electronic base, and with it a new emphasis on the home as the center of society.[20]

At the 1981 ALA Annual Conference, the Library and Information Technology Association held a two-day session on "The Office in the Home: The Support Role of the Library." The session included consideration of "What Should Libraries Plan for in Anticipation of the Electronic Cottage?" Events of this nature are expected to be harbingers of the effort that will characterize ALA during the next two decades. ALA will assert its leadership role for the profession in an effort to reach out to the new technologies and wrestle them into submission through competent use of them, and it will develop guidelines for library support systems. This will be a significant reversal of a past characteristic. In the past, the profession as a whole has demonstrated a lack of interest in really keeping up with the development of the new technologies.

During the next two decades, ALA will increasingly reach out to embrace the new technologies. It will promote their use to handle the avalanche of information that will have continued to increase. In order to handle this growth, it will exercise leadership in collaboration with other associations in gaining policy control over new technological developments so that libraries will operate in the technological age with their eyes wide open.

One way in which the association will take an active leadership role in the development of automated library activities and systems will be to provide expert consultants to work with individual libraries and systems in determining guidelines and standards most appropriate for individual, statewide, and regional programs. Consultant help will be available to assist libraries when it is feasible to invest in new technologies and will advise on compatible formats.

ALA will also promote the use of new technologies by demonstration of their capabilities. It will be a regular feature of major ALA conventions that key events will be broadcasted by satellite for two-way audio, one/two-way video to cable viewing stations in libraries across the nation, so that no one will be denied learning opportunities because of geographical isolation or financial limitations. In order for such programming to be technically sophisticated and programmatically interactive, the Association will need, as members of the headquarters staff, a communications specialist and assistants. This communications staff will work directly with public satellite groups and the local libraries to ensure that their work before, during, and after broadcasts is effective. To this end, guidelines will be developed, including appropriate means for evaluation. Help will be available on cost analysis of programs and on ways of gaining community financial support for programming.

The next video revolution has already arrived in the form of the videodisc. It is the view of competent authorities that:

> . . . The videodisc is more than a communications gadget. It can truly revolutionize television as we now understand it. The reason is not the high quality of picture and sound. It is, rather, the fact that this instrument is *user-controlled*.[21]

The videodisc can serve professional needs on the demand of the user. Programs can be chosen by the user and can be started or stopped at the user's convenience. Random access vidodisc players can randomly access any of the 54,000 frames on one side of a disc in less than five seconds. This is possible because each frame has an identity number (an electronic address). Because there is "segment and still-frame access" (a unique interactivity capability of optical videodisc), the potential is present to change radically the nature of TV viewing, which in the past has been completely passive. The intellectual capacity of the videodisc is staggering. The contents of the Louvre (every painting, every statue) can be pictured in a single videodisc. Four reference works the size of the *Encyclopedia Britannica* will also fit into a single videodisc (one page per frame). The educational potential of the videodisc is limitless.

I envision ALA seeking, during the next two decades and with the aid of its communications specialist and his/her staff, opportunities to cooperate with specialists in the field to produce learning materials which in themselves will be able to further the use of all new technologies that are developing. An example of this type of collaboration is the production of *SchoolDisc*,[22] a cooperative venture of the National Foundation for the

Improvement of Education, the National Education Association, and the American Broadcasting Company. Along with the video production of *SchoolDisc*, publications are regularly issued to enhance the value of *SchoolDisc* programming (e.g., discussion guides, bibliographies).

The U.S. Army has pioneered in using the videodisc as a major training aid, both for knowledge attainment and for skill development. It has estimated, in precise figures, the cost savings over previous direct person-to-person training methods. Tests show that learning through this medium is just as effective as that accomplished in traditional classrooms and skill sessions.

With the continuing emphasis on energy conservation, ALA will, I am sure, recognize that for the continuing education of its members—whether for continuing in their present areas of specialization or for developing new skills in keeping with the new potentials presented by developing technologies or for developing new professional roles—the videodisc presents an unprecedented opportunity to engage in quality distance learning. Home study proponents around the world have for a long time maintained that this method of learning combined with new media makes possible for the first time in history a planned, directed, and systematic program of further education for everyone during his/her entire life.[23] Use of the videodisc with its very specialized capacities makes this affirmation of the potential value and use of home study (distance learning) an exciting and feasible avenue for preventing the obsolescence of the professional segments of our society.

In conclusion, there are extensive opportunities before ALA to take a leadership role in interactive planning with other organizations and groups in demonstrating the possibilities of combining advanced hardware, software, and communications technology in networking and delivery of services so that all functions of libraries—archival, educational, cultural, recreational, informational, and research—serve users in dynamic and practical ways. From the library point of view, many new professional positions will emerge which hold the potential to increase the humanization of librarianship. As the public concurrently experiences more and more success in getting services they need for better, more successful living in this information age, the perceived value of libraries will increase. This, in turn, will lead to a steadier and firmer economic support for libraries. I believe with Fredrick G. Kilgour that technology "is moving librarianship into another of its great ages."[24]

However, in participating in and encouraging the use of technology, I hope that ALA will be an organization which heeds Irving Klempner's warning to librarians and information professionals:

> . . . We cannot escape personal responsibility for assuring that not only our professional expertise but our perceptions as human beings

have been included in the basic design process. . . . The information professional may be the only individual fully aware of a system's strengths and weaknesses, of a system's potential for good or evil. . . . It would seem irresponsible for an information professional not to consider and weigh carefully the overall human and social implications of decisions affecting system design and its services. The quantification, detachment, and objectivity called for in modern science cannot mitigate or relieve us of our responsibility.[25]

It is a responsibility in which ALA needs to be involved as a leader of the profession. Along the same lines, let me quote a remarkable passage from the writings of Alfred North Whitehead:

Modern science has imposed on humanity the necessity for wandering. Its progressive thought and its progressive technology make the transition through time, from generation to generation, a true migration into uncharted seas of adventure. The very benefit of wandering is that it is dangerous and needs skill to avert evils. We must expect, therefore, that the future will disclose dangers. It is the business of the future to be dangerous; and it is among the merits of science that it equips the future for its duties. The prosperous middle classes, who ruled the nineteenth century, placed an excessive value upon the placidity of existence. They refused to face the necessities for social reform imposed by the new industrial system, and they are now refusing to face the necessities for intellectual reform imposed by the new knowledge. The middle class pessimism over the future of the world comes from a confusion between civilization and security. In the immediate future there will be less security than in the immediate past, less stability. It must be admitted that there is a degree of instability which is inconsistent with civilization. But, on the whole, the great ages have been unstable ages.[26]

Whitehead wrote this in 1925; his remarks are, I think, still pertinent today—possibly more so.

HEIGHTENING "LIBRARY AWARENESS"

The American Library Association has as its basic concern, according to its mission statement, "promoting and improving library service and librarianship." One way to achieve this objective is to heighten the general public's "library awareness." Resounding testimony of the importance of increasing the awareness of libraries was evidenced in the resolutions of the 1979 White House Conference, which included as one of the goals and objectives heightened public awareness and which set forth 11 resolutions relating to this.

Heading the list of resolutions was the "development and implementation of an aggressive, comprehensive, nationwide public awareness campaign."[27] The stated objective relating to public awareness in the West Virginia five-year Long Range State Program might well serve as the objective in this area for ALA. It is:

> . . . Eliminate any unfortunate public apathy and replace it with an attitude of unquestioned public need.[28]

Budgeting texts emphasize that the value that the public perceives in services has a direct relationship to the amount of funding those services receive. The program statement in the West Virginia document points out this relationship:

> The value of a strong public library system is dependent upon the breadth of its usage. Many libraries suffer from minimal public support because of a failure to generate a local atmosphere which identifies the library as a public asset of incalculable value. Included in this statewide effort will be individualized programs to meet the specific requirements of various identity groups.[29]

The foregoing statement suggests one of the avenues that ALA will take toward broader participation by the public in developing library programs customized to given groups' particular needs. The early success of *A Planning Process for Public Libraries*[30] indicates that the Public Library Association and other divisions/units of the ALA will base their service roles (in relation to the constituencies they serve) on the actual needs and wants of their particular constituencies. During the next two decades, ALA will use its public information office to focus attention on the activities of assertive library systems, which will aid in providing accountability for the funding the libraries will receive. Roger Greer has defined an assertive library system as one that:

> . . . begins outside the library by identifying needs and interests unsatisfied or unserved by other community agencies. The design of the library system is oriented to specifically serve these needs and extends into the community by delivering services at the points where the information needs originate, whenever possible.[31]

Assertive library service calls for the utilization of new technology to customize user services. It flourishes best when built on interactive planning, which is described by Margaret Monroe as planning between librarians and their special publics "for whom (and with whom) the service is being designed."[32] In other words, a service design cannot be "superimposed" on the public it is to serve: The entire community must be involved in the entire planning process, including identification of interests, wants, and needs. And, any system developed needs to be openended so that other services can be added as needs and awareness grow.

I believe that, during the next two decades, ALA will take an increasing leadership role in demonstrating to libraries what can be accomplished through heightened public awareness. Four factors cited by the White House Conference on Library and Information Services should convince the profession that now is a good time to emphasize this matter of awareness: (1) increased political power, which tends to yield increased funding; (2) enhanced citizen capacity to realize and solve individual problems and needs, (3) a society prepared to deal with change; and (4) a climate which stimulates cultural advancement.[33] I envision that ALA will find ways to demonstrate that libraries support, underpin, influence, and shape the fiber of the nation and are the biggest value that the public gets for its tax dollars. When citizens in every town, county, and city in the nation view the library as central to the educational, social, and cultural development of this nation, then we will know that ''library awareness'' has been achieved.

STRENGTH OF UNITY

As I think about the past of American librarianship and dream about its future, a multitude of pictures come to my mind. Perhaps the one that comes to me most often and stays with me longest is that of the frontier, where we *should* be but tend not to be. Another is suggested by an old hymn:

Follow, follow the gleam . . .

Yes, we need to perceive the gleam and follow it; but I hope that the profession—and particularly our national association—will, so to speak, *supply* the gleam, so we will not be forever chasing after such will-o'-the-wisps as beckon us hither and yon. Let me close by sharing with you still another picture, one which a colleague shared with me just recently. It is evoked by the closing lines of ''The Buried Life,'' a poem by Matthew Arnold:

And there arrives a lull in the hot race
Wherein he doth for ever chase
That flying and elusive shadow, rest.
An air of coolness plays upon his face,
And an unwonted calm pervades his breast.
And then he thinks he knows
The hills where his life rose,
And the sea where it goes.

These lines suggest to me that one of things leadership can do—and indeed *must* do, if it is to be other than fireworks—is to help us see the unity and continuity of our lives—as individuals, as a profession, as an organization;

in short, to remind us of our roots and to fix our gaze upon our destiny. They recall—at least for me—the world of Jewett, Dewey, and Winsor and at the same time point to the twenty-first century.

REFERENCES

1. George Burwell Utley, *The Librarians Conference of 1853: A Chapter of American Library History* (Chicago, IL: American Library Association, 1951), p. 40.

2. "The Proceedings" (of the Conference of Libraries, Philadelphia, October, 1876), *American Library Journal* I (November 30, 1876): 140.

3. Charles Seymour Thompson, *Evolution of the American Public Library,* 1653–1876 (Washington, DC: Scarecrow Press, 1952), p. 220.

4. Cyril O. Houle, *Continuing Learning in the Professions* (San Francisco: Jossey-Bass, 1980), pp. 155–57.

5. William S. Learned, *The American Public Library and the Diffusion of Knowledge* (New York: Harcourt, Brace, 1924), p. 69.

6. *ALA Handbook of Organization 1980–81 and Membership Directory* (Chicago, IL: American Library Association, 1980), p. 1.

7. Houle, p. 158.

8. Malcolm Knowles, "Model for Assessing Continuing Education Needs for a Profession," in *Proceedings of First CLENE Assembly*, Chicago, Illinois, January 23–24, 1976 (Washington, DC: Continuing Library Education Network and Exchange, 1976), p. 84.

9. David G. Brown, *Leadership Vitality: A Workbook for Academic Administrators* (Washington, DC: American Council on Education, 1979), pp. 51–55.

10. Merry Falconer, "Power versus Participation: The New Leadership Style. An Interview with Michael Maccoby," *Leadership* 1 (December, 1980): 19.

11. Edward Holley, *Final Report, Special Committee to Review Program Assessment and Procedures* (Chicago, IL: American Library Association, 1981), p. 4.

12. Wayne A. Lemburg, "Charting the Future through Strategic Planning," *Association Management* (October 1980): 151.

13. Alvin Toffler, *The Third Wave* (New York: Bantam Books, 1981), pp. 194–207.

14. Houle, p. 154.

15. Lemburg, p. 155.

16. Knowles, pp. 84–85.

17. Houle, p. 27.

18. Houle, pp. 35–74.

19. Houle, pp. 305–15.

20. Toffler, p. 210.

21. John Ciampa, "The Video Disc: Its Effect on Programming," *Television Quarterly* 17 (Winter 1980–81): 24.

22. *SchoolDisc* (Washington, DC: National Foundation for the Improvement of Education, 1981).

23. Karlheimz Rebel, "The Necessity of Further Education in the Professions and Home Study as a Means of Realization," *Convergence* 3 (January 1970): 66–74.

24. Frederick G. Kilgour, "The Impact of Techology on Libraries," in *The Information Society: Issues and Answers; the American Library Association's Presidential Commission for the 1977 Detroit Annual Conference*, ed. E. J. Josey (Phoenix, AZ: Oryx Press, 1978), p. 18.

25. Irving M. Klempner, "Information Technology and Personal Responsibility," *Special Libraries* 72 (April 1981): 162.

26. Alfred North Whitehead, *Science and the Modern World* (New York: Macmillan, 1931), pp. 298–99.

27. *The White House Conference on Library and Information Services—1979, The Final Report Summary* (Washington, DC: National Commission on Libraries and Information Science, 1980), pp. 45–47.

28. West Virginia Library Commission, *Long Range State Program 1981–1986* (Charleston, WV: West Virginia Library Commission, 1981), p. 28.

29. West Virginia Library Commission, p. 25.

30. Vernon E. Palmour, Marcia D. Bellassai, and Nancy V. De Wath, *A Planning Process for Public Libraries* (Chicago, IL: American Library Association, 1980).

31. Roger C. Greer, "The Public Library Setting—Community Profiles and What the 80s and 90s Will Bring," *Public Libraries and New Directions for Adult Services: An Institute in Honor of Rose Vainstein*, eds. Joan C. Durrance and Rose Vainstein (Ann Arbor, MI: School of Library Science, University of Michigan, 1981), p. 25.

32. Margaret E. Monroe, "The Future for Public Library Adult Services, Opportunities and New Directions," *Public Libraries and New Directions for Adult Services: An Institute in Honor of Rose Vainstein*, eds.

Joan C. Durrance and Rose Vainstein (Ann Arbor, MI: School of Library Science, University of Michigan, 1981), p. 61.

33. *The White House Conference on Library and Information Services—1979,* p. 45.

Index

Compiled by Fred Ramey